AF378935

Reconstructing Cezanne

Cezanne Reconstructing

Sequence and Process
in Paul Cezanne's works on paper

LUXEMBOURG & DAYAN

Ridinghouse

Contents

Paul Cezanne:
The Introduction of a New Art

WALTER FEILCHENFELDT

On 19 January 2019 – the artist's 180th birthday – the catalogue raisonné of Cezanne's work was launched online. This catalogue, which lists all his paintings, watercolours and drawings, was preceded by four others: Lionello Venturi's *Cézanne: Son art – son œuvre* (1936), Adrien Chappuis' *The Drawings of Paul Cézanne* (1973), and John Rewald's *Paul Cézanne: The Watercolours* (1983) and *The Paintings of Paul Cézanne* (1996). Two important monographs should also be noted: *Cézanne und das Ende der wissenschaftlichen Perspektive* (Cézanne and the End of Scientific Perspective; 1938) by Fritz Novotny and *Cézanne and the End of Impressionism* by Richard Shiff (1984). But why talk of 'the end' when Cezanne marks new beginnings? It is no coincidence that his successors, like Picasso and Matisse, referred to him as 'the father of us all'. Alberto Giacometti said that there had never been a day when he did not think about Cezanne. Why do artists like Lucian Freud, Bridget Riley, Jasper Johns and Richard Serra admire Cezanne so much? It is because he paved the way for modern art: he marked the path away from figuration and opened the door to abstraction.

Venturi's catalogue of 1936 bears the classic title *Cézanne: Son art – son œuvre,* and at that time an interpretive essay was an essential part of such a task. Now that we have an online catalogue of the complete works of Cezanne, including all known material by him, the time has come for another interpretive essay and to take a closer look at his work in light of the new information that has been compiled in the intervening decades.

While it would be difficult to separate the artwork from what it represents in Cezanne's paintings, many of his watercolours and drawings, however much they may still possess figurative elements, are less concerned with depicting a motif than with a composition shaped by it: patches of colour, lines and planes that come together to form a conceptual structure. When Cezanne copied sculptures by Puget or Houdon in the Louvre, it was not their artistic message that interested him. They served him merely as a pretext for his art, to practise the two-dimensional representation of three-dimensional models; whether the depiction resembled the model was secondary. By way of an analogy, the different objects depicted in his sketches do not have meaningful relationships to each other, but thanks to the assurance with which the artist arranged the various forms, they combine into a conceptual artwork. His portraits are neither physiognomic nor psychological studies of the sitters: a drawing of Madame Cezanne does not 'resemble' her, even though she is always recognisable.

Cezanne's works on paper, with or without colour, are the outcome of the new artistic concept that he was inventing. Many drawings are so condensed that it is impossible to discern what is represented. Often the paper has been cut and the blank paper has become part of the composition. His works on paper should be framed without mounts because the empty space – empty paper – is part of the work and should not be disturbed by the additional empty paper that a mat would bring.

The online catalogue is done. Now the real work begins, which consists in using the art historical knowledge of our time to analyse the work of this artist who died in 1906.

Reconstructing Cezanne
at Luxembourg & Dayan

YUVAL ETGAR

One of the great joys in a scholar's career is the sense of accomplishment experienced when two pieces of information come together to form a new discovery. Researchers spend much of their lives hoping to confirm that their hypotheses are more than just educated guesses, and that their methods are solid and should be adopted by others. Art history in this respect has always been a particularly difficult field of study, where intuition inevitably, and without exception, plays a decisive role. One of the debates inherent to the discipline can therefore be outlined in the following terms: how does one draw a line between art historical accountability on the one hand, and subjective interpretation on the other? The task is never simple, particularly when considering subjects that are firmly grounded in canonical discourse. The present exhibition and its accompanying book – dedicated to one of the most important artists in the history of art – has given us a rare opportunity to explore new methods of art historical research where forensic analysis of material evidence forms the basis for an engaged and vital critical debate.

The scholarship of Paul Cezanne has proven to be a particularly sensitive expertise, guarded by the high stakes of a competitive market and the small number of dominant scholars who had access to the artist's estate in the century following his death. This is manifested more than anywhere else in the four directories of works that provided a map to the artist's oeuvre until quite recently. Three of these remain the subject of little contention. They include Lionello Venturi's book *Cézanne: Son art – son œuvre* of 1936, and two additional catalogues from 1983 and 1996 dedicated to the artist's watercolours and oils respectively, both written by the renowned American scholar John Rewald. The fourth catalogue, however – written by the French connoisseur Adrien Chappuis in 1973 as the first comprehensive directory of the artist's drawings on paper – has been at the centre of recent scholarly debate. Chappuis was not an academic in the traditional sense of the word. He began his research into the life and work of Paul Cezanne through collecting, most notably his single purchase of 130 sheets of paper with numerous drawings on them at a sale in 1933.[1] Eager to make sense of his new collection, Chappuis was soon faced with a number of difficulties – above all, the fact that none of the drawings were dated by the artist.[2] A thorough and devoted student, Chappuis soon began to draw links with a number of works in other collections, which he studied with growing enthusiasm over the following decades, publishing three books on the subject before the release of his complete catalogue of drawings.[3]

The outcome of Chappuis' project is a commendable and comprehensive directory of drawings (after all, the catalogue includes 1,242 entries, still today representing the vast majority of works in this medium known to us). Yet Chappuis' catalogue raisonné has recently been subject to growing criticism for its methodological approach and its questionable factual credibility in certain respects, particularly with regard to the dating of certain drawings. This critical perspective is nowhere better explained than in Karsten Schubert's article 'Cezanne, Chappuis and the Limits of Connoisseurship', published in *The Burlington Magazine* in 2006.[4] Schubert, also a collector of Cezanne's works on paper, grew more and more critical of Chappuis' commentary when he tried to gather information about works in his own collection, eventually deciding to publicly contest the expert's authority in the field. 'What Chappuis offers in place of a factual approach is one of the great acts of speculation in the field of nineteenth century art history', he wrote, adding that:

> [Chappuis] sets out to establish dates for no less than all 1,400 drawings... Yet he remained completely silent on the way in which he arrived at this phenomenal chronology. He established his sequence 'by giving preference to [his] own feelings and intuition when judging values rather than following a systematically logical approach [...]'. However acute and accurate Chappuis's instincts were, there surely came a point at which it might have been possible for him to put his method into words. At the very least, his instincts must have been based on certain assumptions and observations.[5]

Schubert called for a new, accountable scholarship. His appeal came at an opportune moment, coinciding with a growing tendency among art historians specialising in modernity to rely on empirical, so-called forensic analysis of works.

As much thanks to technological developments as disciplinary ones, art historians over the past two decades have enjoyed increasing access to diverse sources of information – online and otherwise – that enables them to perform comprehensive cross-referencing of historical facts and archival materials and to engage with an extensive network of fellow researchers locally and internationally, in turn setting new standards for scholarly credibility. Moreover, and thanks to the rise of interdisciplinary knowledge, scholars now place far greater weight on scientific analysis of the materials they study; in Cezanne's case, as we shall see, these come into expression in the close examination and comparison of paper brands, watermarks, edges and pigments, among other things. Achieved in combination with certain freedoms that can only be attained thanks to the temporal distance gained from the subject matter, contemporary scholarship is beginning to show Cezanne in a new light. The expressions of such new art historical methodologies are perhaps best represented by the online catalogue raisonné of the artist that was made available to the public in 2019, constantly evolving and receptive to new information and corrections.[6] They are also evident in the recent proliferation of exhibitions focusing on Cezanne from new perspectives and engaged in particular with his works on paper or with his allegedly 'unfinished' paintings as subjects for close analysis. Consider, for example, the exhibitions *The Hidden Cézanne: From Sketchbook to Canvas* at the Kunstmuseum Basel and *Cézanne: Metamorphoses* at the Staatliche Kunsthalle Karlsruhe, both in 2017.

The project *Reconstructing Cezanne: Sequence and Process in Paul Cezanne's Works on Paper* has emerged as part of this new paradigmatic shift. It focuses on one specific expression of the general mood in the field, which can be recognised in the recent findings of the Swiss scholar and curator Fabienne Ruppen. Over the past eight years Ruppen has been dedicated to the study of Cezanne's works on paper and the cataloguing of the artist's oeuvre based on close examination of the paper types that he used for his drawings and watercolours. By analysing the watermarks embedded into certain papers or examining the edges of the sheets, Ruppen has been able to identify works that originate from single sketchbooks or paper blocks, or even as parts of a single sheet of paper that was split by the artist in advance of starting work.[7] Ruppen's reconstructions not only help us to rectify certain errors concerning the dating of works, but their outcomes have far-reaching implications for the interpretation of Cezanne's practice, linking works that were never compared hitherto because they failed, for example, to show a clear thematic relationship to one another. Thus a watercolour depiction of a landscape might demonstrate similar pictorial concerns to those of a portrait or a still life.

Indeed, the exhibition *Reconstructing Cezanne* is focused entirely on manifestations of Ruppen's methodology as it comes into expression in landscape drawings and watercolour paintings, but the principle applies to any other genre that Cezanne engaged with, as well as across different genres. Consider for example the horizontal orientation of lines and the empty spaces left by Cezanne in a watercolour such as *Le Jardin des Lauves: vue sur Aix et la Cathédrale de Saint-Sauveur* from 1902–06 (cat.5b, p.37, included in the exhibition), and compare these traits with those of a still life watercolour such as *Bouteille, carafe, cruche et citrons*, from the same years (fig.1). Thematically disconnected from one another, these two works have firm grounds for comparison thanks to the analysis of watermarks, which enables us to recognise them as part of a wider group produced in a particular time and on a particular type of paper (in this case, one that was manufactured in the famous mills of Saint-Marcel-lès-Annonay in the French *département* of Ardèche). Naturally, such lines of inquiry, seeking continuity between one work and another based on formal concerns, have already been widely acknowledged in cases where Cezanne worked on both sides of a single sheet of paper. *Le garçon au gilet rouge I* of 1889–90 (fig.2a), whose unusually long limbs are mirrored in a study of a Hercules sculpture by Puget on the verso of the paper (fig.2b), boasting similar characteristics, offers a case in point. Broader analysis of sequence and process in the artist's work, however, is still lacking. Forensic study of paper affinities can show that a group of works undoubtedly emerged from one batch of paper, confirming suspicions regarding the formal concerns of colour, shape and rhythm that motivated Cezanne to proceed from one work to another, and clarifying in what way he went about such transitions.

While undoubtedly innovative in its approach, Ruppen's work nevertheless has roots in a certain school of art historical scholarship that has been engaged with similar technical methods of research. Focusing on the close analysis of Cezanne's production processes or materials for nearly a century now, this branch of study had limited resources at its disposal until quite recently and thus remained somewhat peripheral to the canon. Examples of such work can be traced back as far as Roger Fry's excellent study on Cezanne's development from 1927, and more directly to Robert Ratcliffe's thesis on 'Cezanne's working methods and their theoretical background' from 1960,[8] whose influence was primarily evident among those generations of students who studied under Ratcliffe at the Courtauld Institute of Art in London. In an attempt to widen the exposure of this branch of Cezanne scholarship, *Reconstructing Cezanne* focuses on a narrow portion of Ruppen's theoretical research and aims to translate its implications from textual terms into spatial and visual ones. By examining a small selection of works that are materially linked to one another, we hope to offer evidence as to the potential of such readings – or, better yet, viewings – of a particular body of work based on reconstructive methodology.

The path to *Reconstructing Cezanne* was not simple. With more than five major institutional exhibitions dedicated to Paul Cezanne opening in Europe and the United States in the coming two years alone, we were met

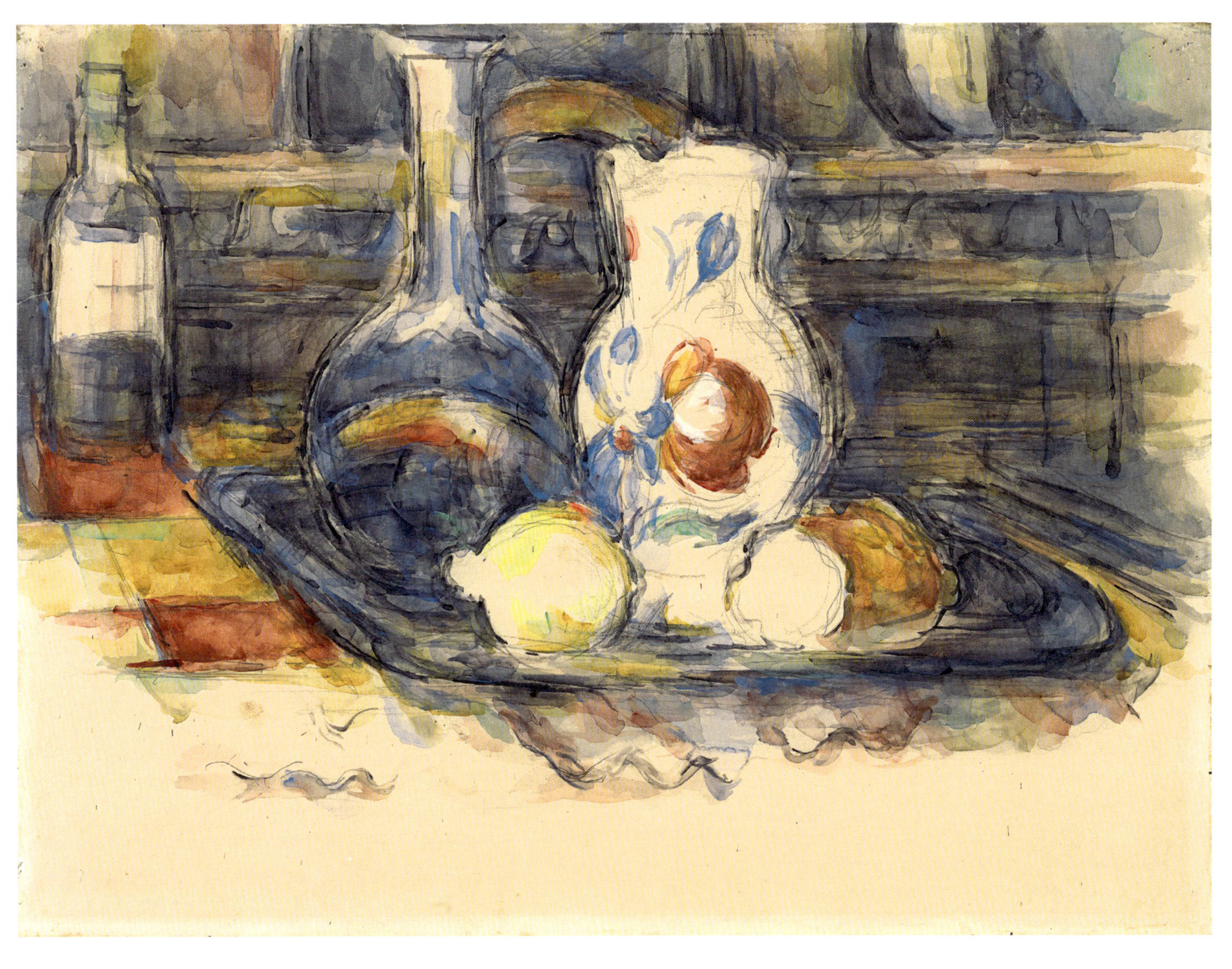

Fig.1
Bouteille, carafe, cruche et citrons, 1902–06
Graphite, watercolour, and gouache on wove paper, 17⁹⁄₁₆ × 23⁵⁄₈ in. (44.5 × 60 cm)
Museo Thysssen-Bornemisza, Madrid

13

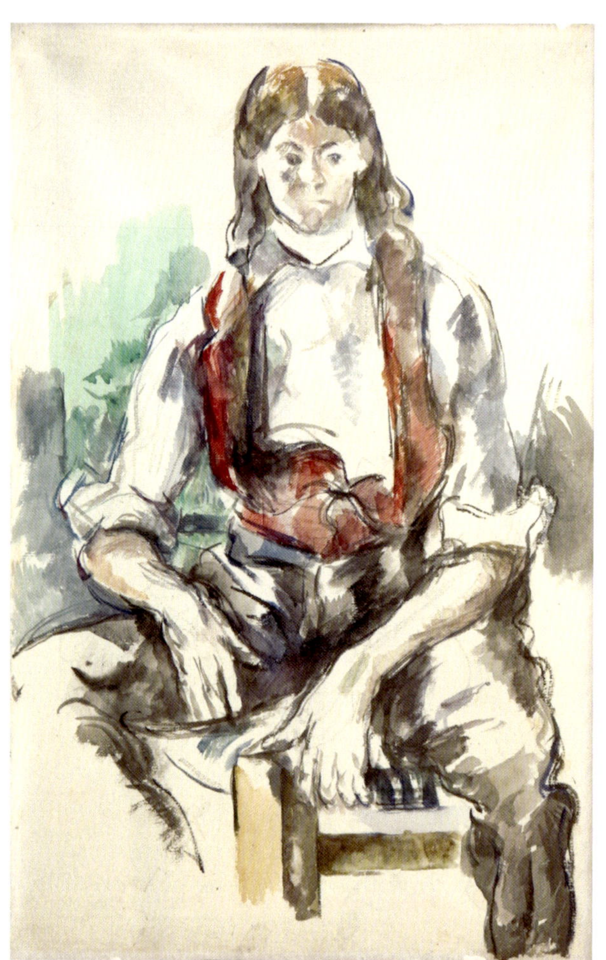

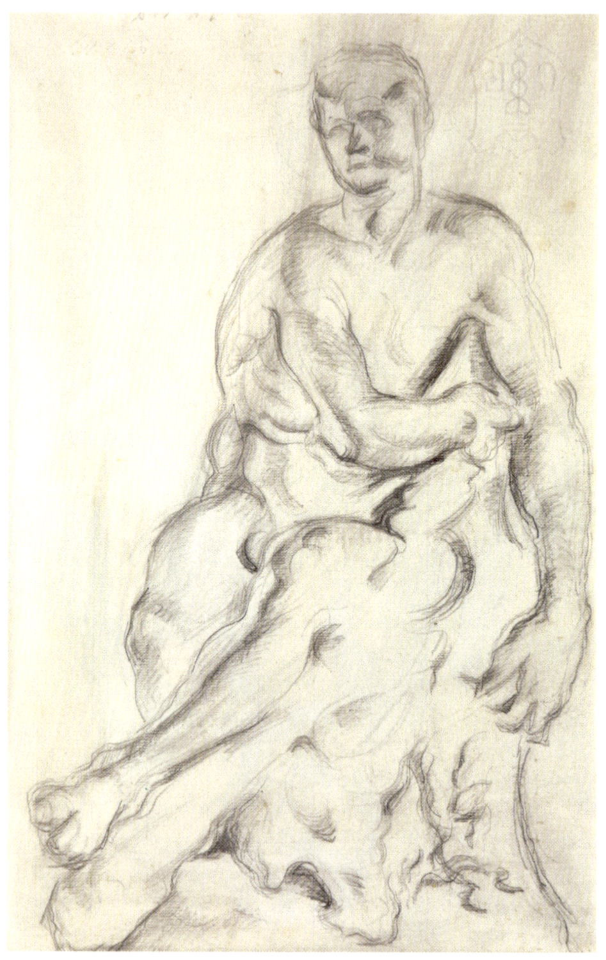

Fig.2a (recto)
Le garçon au gilet rouge, I, 1889–90
Graphite and watercolour on laid paper,
19 × 12³⁄₁₆ in. (46 × 31 cm)
Private collection

Fig.2b (verso)
D'après Puget: Hercule au repos, 1884–87
Graphite on laid paper,
18⅛ × 12³⁄₁₆ in. (46 × 31 cm)
Private collection

with challenges at every step of the way. But we also came to expand our network of relations with colleagues and supporters whose dedication to the field was overwhelming and contagious. Walter Feilchenfeldt, one of the world's leading Cezanne experts and co-author of the artist's online catalogue raisonné, has guided us from the first stages of the project all the way to its realisation. He also introduced us to Philippe Cezanne, the artist's great-grandson, who provided important insights into the artist's biography, and to Fabienne Ruppen, whose dedication to the subject has not only been inspirational but forced us to employ rigorous conditions of selection when we set out to look for works. It is perhaps thanks to Ruppen's uncompromising approach to the subject that a number of world-leading institutions have given their support to our project and lent us drawings and watercolours of the highest quality. *Reconstructing Cezanne* includes loans from the Fondation Beyeler in Basel, the Ashmolean Museum in Oxford, Musée Granet in Aix-en-Provence, and the Courtauld Institute of Art in London. We are honoured to include works from such prominent collections in our show as well as those of the private collectors who asked to remain anonymous. The Courtauld Institute of Art in particular not only loaned us one of the most important works in the exhibition, but some of its finest faculty members joined us in conversation and discussion along the way, offering us critical insights. Finally, we had the privilege to collaborate with Ridinghouse as our co-publishers on this occasion. We thank our editor Sophie Kullmann and designer Mark Thomson for their exceptional and devoted work. We would not have had the privilege of publishing this book together if it wasn't for the late gallerist and publisher Karsten Schubert, who, over the last months of his life became our adviser to the exhibition and more importantly, a close friend. We dedicate this publication to him.

1 Chappuis bought the majority of his Cezanne drawings from the dealer Paul Guillaume around 1933. Many of these, as well as other works on paper by Cezanne include more than one drawing, and at times they are executed both on the recto and the verso of the sheet. Indeed, some of the works that were discovered only after the publication of Chappuis' catalogue raisonné were on the verso of sheets previously examined by him.

2 Cezanne rarely signed his works and even more rarely dated them. This is true of his watercolours and drawings as well as his oils.

3 Chappuis' three interim publications, serving as preparatory studies for his catalogue raisonné, comprise *Dessins de Paul Cézanne* (1938), analysing 52 examples from Chappuis' own collection; *Dessins de Cézanne*, published in 1957 and including additional examples; and a two-volume publication on the Cezanne drawings in the collection of the Kunstmuseum Basel, published in 1962 (and forming the first complete catalogue of the museum's holdings).

4 Schubert's article was in fact commissioned by *The Burlington Magazine* as part of a special issue dedicated to Cezanne, marking the occasion of the artist's exhibition at the National Gallery in London that year.

5 Karsten Schubert, 'Cézanne, Chappuis and the Limits of Connoisseurship', *The Burlington Magazine*, vol.148, no.1242, special issue on Paul Cézanne (1839–1906), September 2006, pp.612–20.

6 Walter Feilchenfeldt, Jayne Warman and David Nash (eds), *The Paintings, Watercolors and Drawings of Paul Cezanne: An Online Catalogue Raisonné*, www.cezannecatalogue.com/catalogue/index.php.

7 So far, of the 2,100 officially recognised to date, Ruppen has reviewed and analysed in person more than 1,400 Cezanne works on paper.

8 Roger Eliot Fry, *Cézanne: A Study of His Development*, Hogarth Press, London, 1927; Robert William Ratcliffe, *Cézanne's Working Methods and their Theoretical Background*, University of London, London, 1960.

Tackling Cezanne's Paper:
On the Reconstruction of Loose Sheets

FABIENNE RUPPEN

The Montagne Sainte-Victoire rises majestically behind a plain studded
with pine trees in Paul Cezanne's watercolour of the same name in the
collection of the Courtauld Institute of Art in London (cat.1, p.18).[1] The
mountain is a landmark of the area around Aix-en-Provence, where the
artist was born in 1839 and where he spent most of his life. Cezanne began
this composition with a loose graphite sketch, giving equal weight to
hatching and contour line and going into just enough detail to allow it to
stand on its own without the addition of watercolour. While the brush
follows the pencil to a large extent, filling in the different planes delineated
in graphite, there are also areas where watercolour and graphite are used in
isolation. The result is a carefully balanced arrangement of line and colour.
Cezanne favoured local colour, especially shades of blue and green, which
he complemented with red, orange and yellow highlights. It is the latter
that gives this view its freshness and luminosity.

When we look beyond the image, we are struck by the uneven edges of
the sheet, especially the noticeable bulge on the torn lower edge close to the
left corner. In the interest of achieving an immaculate presentation, it is
common practice to 'fix' such 'damage' or to cover it up with a mount. This
often hides important information or even obliterates it. Yet coffee stains
and fly specks can lead us to the studio where a sheet of paper was stored;
tears and splashes can conjure up the artist in front of his motif. Rather
than treat these marks as defects, we should learn to look at them as clues.[2]
And, indeed, thanks to the distinctive torn edge of the Courtauld half-sheet
I have been able to identify the second half of the original full sheet in
another collection (cat.2, p.19).[3] The find is significant as it is the first time
the two halves of a divided Cezanne sheet have been reunited.[4]

The other half of the sheet also shows a landscape: a panorama with
a rolling plain in the foreground and a low mountain range behind it. In
the middle ground, houses dotted here and there and clumps of trees look
like children's building blocks. Four central architectural structures – two
of them no more than rudimentary suggestions – form a diamond shape
that is repeated in the diagonal arrangement of fields in the foreground.
While the precise location of the landscape in *Paysage provençal* has not yet
been established, it is assumed to be somewhere around Aix.[5] Since the bulk
of Cezanne's landscapes originated in this area, and the two watercolours
do not show the same view, they were never discussed as related until the
discovery of their material connection. The reconstruction of the full sheet,
however, reveals similarities ranging from the palette and the ratio of
graphite to watercolour to the compositional conception.

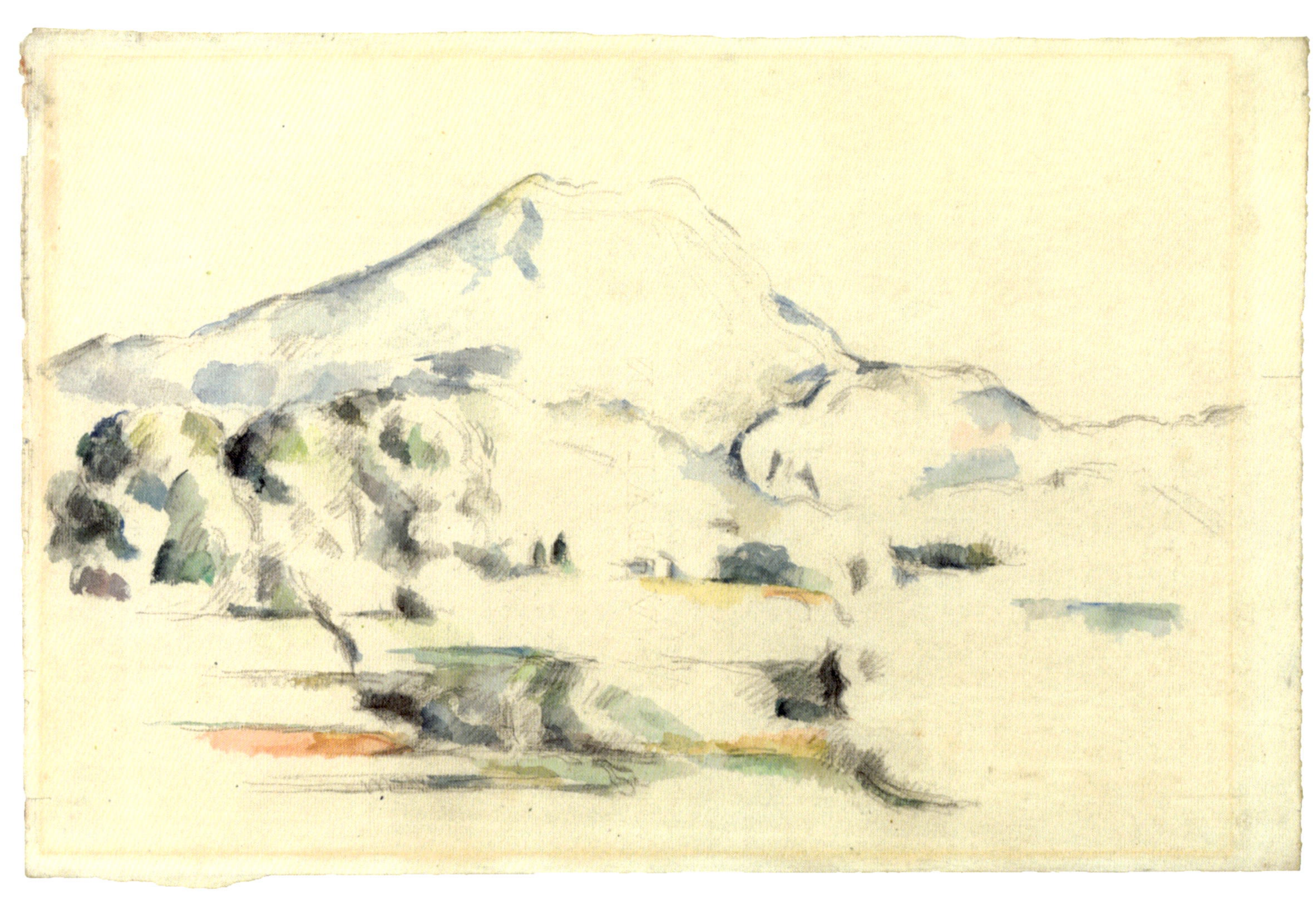

Cat.1
Paul Cezanne (1839–1906)
La Montagne Sainte-Victoire, 1885–87
Graphite and watercolour on laid paper, 12⅞ × 19⅞ in. (32.7 × 50.5 cm)
The Courtauld Gallery, London (The Samuel Courtauld Trust)

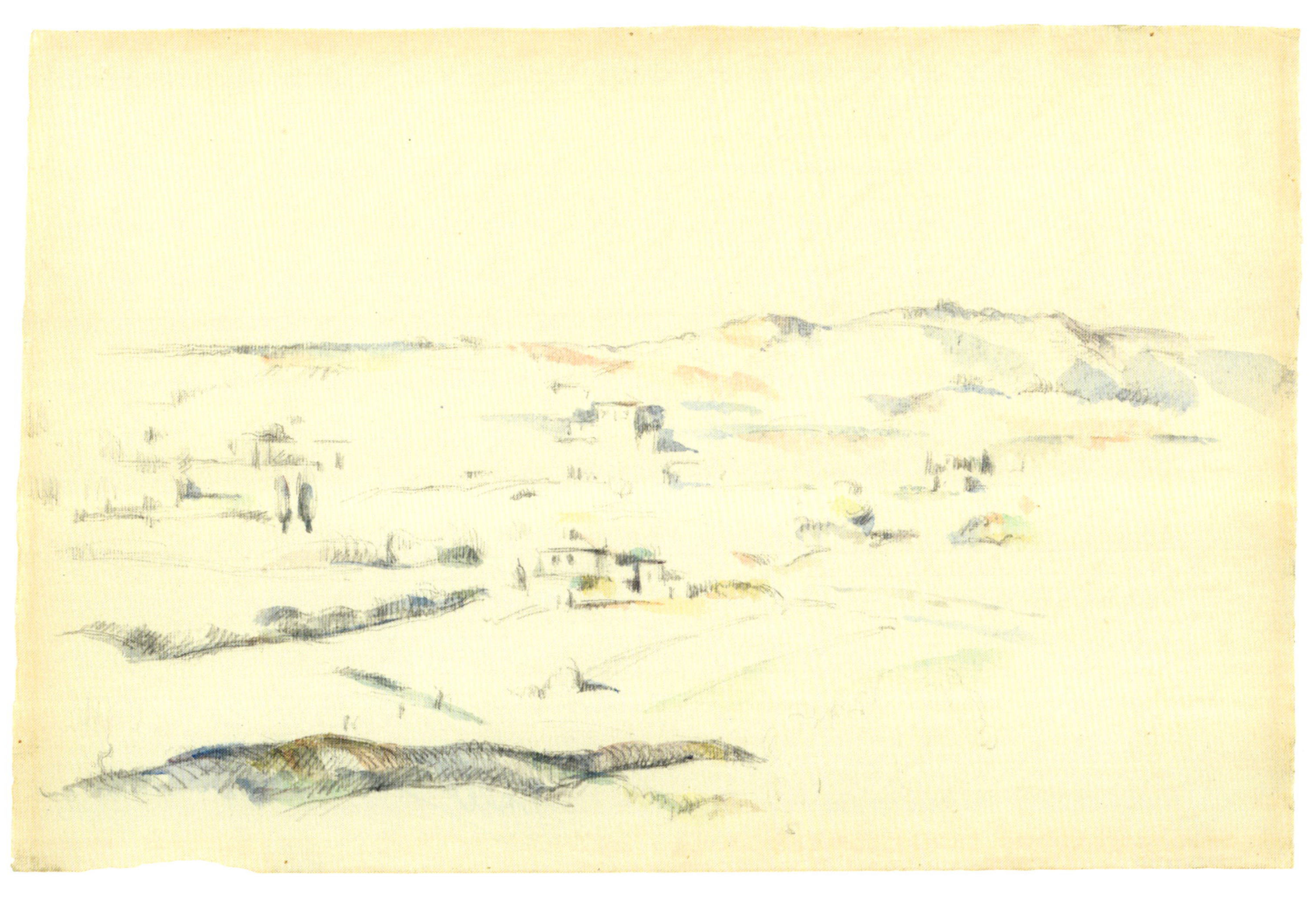

Cat.2
Paul Cezanne (1839–1906)
Paysage provençal (environs de Gardanne?), c.1885
Graphite and watercolour on laid paper, 12⅝ × 19¾ in. (32.1 × 50.3 cm)
Private collection

The juxtaposition of the two watercolours in the exhibition offers a rare opportunity to look at some of Cezanne's works on loose sheets in their original context. A selection of complementary works that are closely related in terms of material demonstrates that knowledge of this context stimulates cross-genre as well as cross-media comparisons which ultimately facilitate not only a deeper understanding of each individual work but also of the artist's oeuvre as a whole. This case study demonstrates the potential of the support – hitherto rarely taken into account by art historians – as a source for the study of works on paper in general. Prerequisite for this is the systematic recording and evaluation of paper qualities and signs of use.

Reconstructing Cezanne's Paper Supports

Very few of Cezanne's drawings and watercolours have come down to us in their original context. Executors of the artist's estate, art dealers and collectors broke up most of his sketchbooks to sell as individual sheets. To maximise profits, study sheets with several clearly separate images were also cut up.[6] Assessing the quality and condition of the paper support is crucial to any reconstruction of the original material units. Traces of stitching or binding, pinholes or grease stains left by oleaginous binders allow for the partial reconstruction of sketchbooks that once contained some 990 works – that is, almost half of the 2,100 drawings and water-colours by Cezanne known to survive.[7] Different criteria apply to the roughly 40 works executed on everyday papers such as lined writing paper or the versos of plates taken from various publications and repurposed as supports. In the latter case, tracing their origin sheds light on Cezanne's reading material. Moreover, the date of publication provides a *terminus post quem* for the works in question.[8] Yet another set of criteria applies to the bulk of his drawing and watercolours – some 1,070 – executed not in sketchbooks or on everyday sheets of paper but, like the two watercolours described earlier, on loose sheets of drawing paper. Closer examination reveals that he favoured a French standard format, the so-called *raisin*, measuring approximately 48 by 63 centimetres. But he rarely worked on the whole sheet, preferring instead to halve it, as he did in the case of *Montagne Sainte-Victoire* and *Paysage provençal*; the half-sheets thus measure approximately 48 by 31.5 centimetres.[9]

Irregular torn edges like the ones mentioned here suggest that Cezanne used a bone folder and knife himself, and it is tempting to picture him at work preparing his sheets. In the case of those half-sheets with watercolour reaching all the way to the margin, narrow paint-free strips along the torn edge – caused by the freshly cut paper fibres standing on end – indicate that he usually cut the sheets only just before he set to work. Whether he did this in the studio or *sur le motif* is another question, but it is likely that the cutting was done whenever he actually needed a sheet of paper. We can also assume that for practical reasons he used the two halves of any one sheet in rapid succession. This suggests that the depictions on the two halves are close to each other in terms of date and place of execution. Reuniting loose sheets therefore promises not only insights into Cezanne's creative process but also new clues that can help to date and identify motifs. The technical and stylistic parallels between the Courtauld *Montagne Sainte-Victoire* and its pendant, the *Paysage provençal* in a private collection, corroborate this assumption. However, the sheer number of loose sheets in Cezanne's oeuvre and the fact that many of these have subsequently been trimmed and straightened makes such an endeavour extremely difficult if not impossible. To reconstruct former units we thus need other criteria, which have also served as the basis for the selection of the works shown in this exhibition.

The key differentiator between the loose sheets is the variation in paper quality. Nineteenth-century artists had the choice between laid paper and wove paper (*papier vergé* and *papier vélin*). The characteristic ribbed texture of laid paper is the result of the wire sieve used in its fabrication: narrowly spaced parallel horizontal wires (laid lines) are crossed by more widely spaced vertical wires (chain lines). As the excess water drains from the fibre pulp, the wire sieve imparts its distinctive pattern to the sheet of paper. Wove paper, on the other hand, is made with a fine-meshed woven sieve, resulting in paper with a much smoother surface.[10] Moreover, the technical advances of industrialisation had given rise to the production of a much wider range of paper and, by the second half of the nineteenth century, to an unprecedented variety of drawing paper. Not only was paper now available in numerous formats and tints, it also came with different surface treatments that allowed artists to control the speed at which liquid drawing media were absorbed.

Watermarks were first introduced in the thirteenth century to distinguish different kinds of paper. Applied during the manufacturing process, they can identify the owner of the paper mill, its location, the customer of a specific product or the paper's properties and therefore provide important information in the study of loose sheets of drawing paper.[11] Specialist shops offered drawing paper as single sheets or, more cheaply, in bulk (*à la main*) – that is, batches of 25 sheets.[12] It can be assumed that for economic and pragmatic reasons Cezanne bought *à la main*. Unlike some of his contemporaries, for example Georges Seurat (1859–1891), Cezanne was not loyal to any one product, preferring instead to use different manufacturers and paper qualities.[13] Their different watermarks thus help us to reallocate his loose sheets. It is likely, for example, that for practical reasons Cezanne did not store sheets from the same batch for several years but used them within a relatively short span of time. Sheets with the same watermark can therefore be gathered into groups, which can be regarded as units just like sketchbooks or everyday papers.

So far, I have examined some 1,400 of Cezanne's 2,100 works on paper and documented 218 watermarks. What we can see from these figures is that numerous drawing papers used by Cezanne do not bear a watermark. This can be attributed to three reasons. First, by no means all drawing papers had watermarks, even though loose sheets are watermarked significantly more often than sketchbook sheets.[14] Second, Cezanne's habit of cutting sheets in half has led to missing watermarks. Some watermarks stretch over the whole length of the sheet or are centred and thus appear at least partially on both halves, others consist of two parts, the so-called main mark and its countermark, which are often spread over the two halves. But just as often watermarks run along one of the short sides or are placed off-centre so that the second half lacks a watermark once the sheet has been divided. Such a case is represented in the exhibition by *Sentier en forêt*, a watercolour on a laid paper half-sheet (cat.10, p.67).[15] Third, some existing watermarks may have been eliminated when the edges of a sheet were trimmed, as in the case of a wove paper half-sheet titled *Dans la forêt, II* from c.1895–8, whose height has been reduced by 4 centimetres. This retrospectively moved the interior of the forest with undergrowth and rocks into the centre of the paper (cat.9b, p.65).[16] The same is the case with a trimmed wove paper half-sheet showing *Arbres et clôture* (cat.11, p.69).

The 218 documented watermarks can be divided into 32 different types, which according to producer, client and countermark can be attributed to 13 groups.[17] The exhibition brings together 11 loose sheets, which – apart from the three halves without watermarks – belong to three different watermark groups. Close analysis allows us to define the characteristics of these three groups and exemplifies what we might learn from a support-based reallocation of Cezanne's drawings and watercolours.

The *raisin* sheet reconstructed earlier is a piece of laid paper with a two-part wire-formed watermark.[18] Across the centre of the half-sheet with the *Montagne Sainte-Victoire* runs the horizontal main mark, which reads 'VIDALON' in a serif font (fig.3); the half with the *Paysage provençal* bears the corresponding countermark, the equally centrally positioned monogram 'S A V' (fig.4, p.24).[19] Such pairs of watermarks not only provide important clues to finding further matching half-sheets, but they also facilitate the identification of the paper in question and thus the place and time of its production. 'VIDALON' stands for Vidalon-lès-Annonay, a village in the Ardèche where the Ancienne Manufacture run by the Canson and Montgolfier family began making paper in the late seventeenth century.[20] Granted the title of Manufacture Royale in 1784, the Canson et Montgolfier mill was one of the most prestigious producers of a wide range of high-quality paper in Cezanne's time. Sales catalogues of the firm list the 'S A V' monogram in connection with various products, including one that also bears the lettering 'VIDALON'.[21] 'S A V' stands for the Société Anonyme des papeteries de Vidalon, which was founded in December 1880.[22] Paper bearing the monogram is therefore unlikely to have been commercially available before 1881, which establishes a *terminus post quem* – albeit an early one – for the drawings and watercolours Cezanne executed on it.[23] Very few dates need to be corrected on the basis of this finding. Most of Cezanne's works on paper with the 'VIDALON' or 'S A V' watermark have already been assigned to later years in Adrien Chappuis' catalogue raisonné of the drawings and in John Rewald's catalogue of the watercolours, published in 1973 and 1983 respectively.

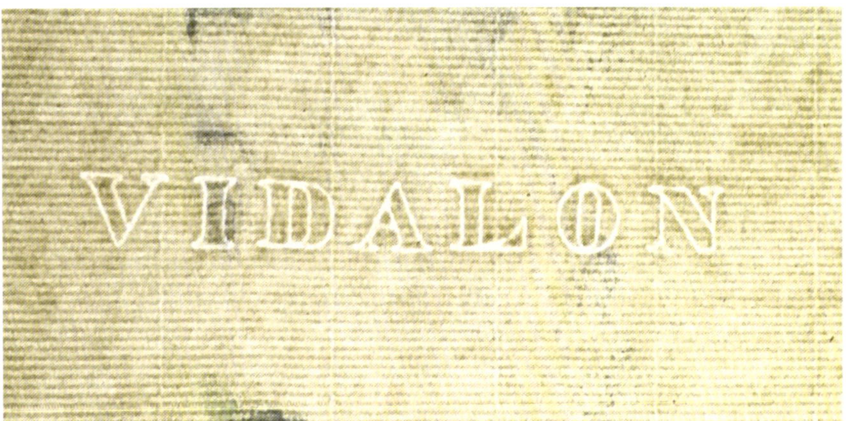

Fig.3
Detail of cat.1, *La Montagne Sainte-Victoire*, 1885–87, showing the wire-formed watermark 'VIDALON' in transmitted light

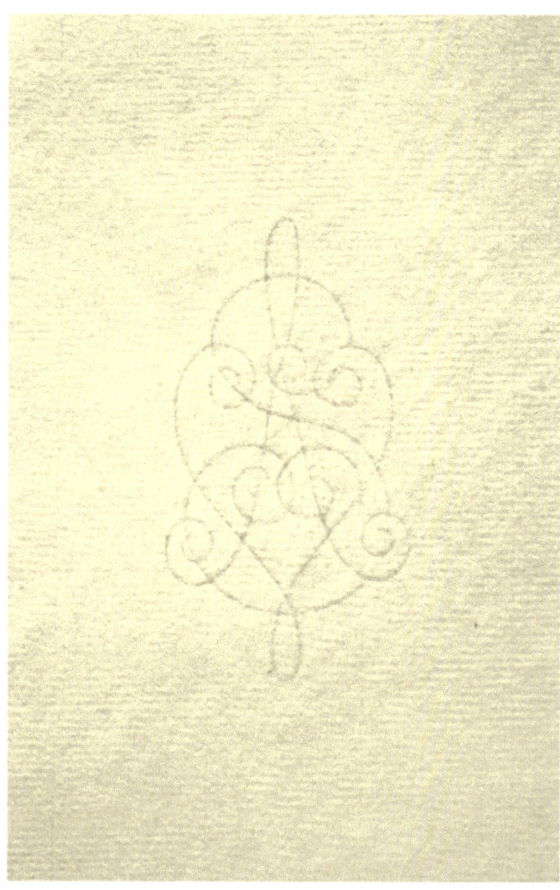

Fig.4
Detail of cat.2, *Paysage provençal (environs de Gardanne?)*, c.1885, showing the wire-formed watermark 'S A V' in natural light

Thus far the monogram countermark has been documented on ten of Cezanne's sheets, the main mark 'VIDALON' on sixteen.[24] With the exception of two fragments, each of the 26 pieces of paper is a half-sheet, with five of them worked on both sides, bringing the total number of works in the group to 31. Interestingly, they feature a limited number of subjects that Cezanne returned to over and over again. One of them is the Montagne Sainte-Victoire, which takes centre stage not only in the Courtauld sheet but also in two watercolours in the collection of the Barnes Foundation in Philadelphia and another one in that of the Musée d'Orsay, Paris (fig.5).[25] The Courtauld view was executed southwest of the Jas de Bouffan, the estate of Cezanne's parents west of Aix, while the three views now in Philadelphia and Paris were painted from a grove east of the terrace of the Château Noir. From 1887 until the completion of his studio at Les Lauves in the hills just north of Aix in 1902, Cezanne stored his materials in a shed in the grounds of this neo-Gothic castle on the road from Aix to Le Tholonet.

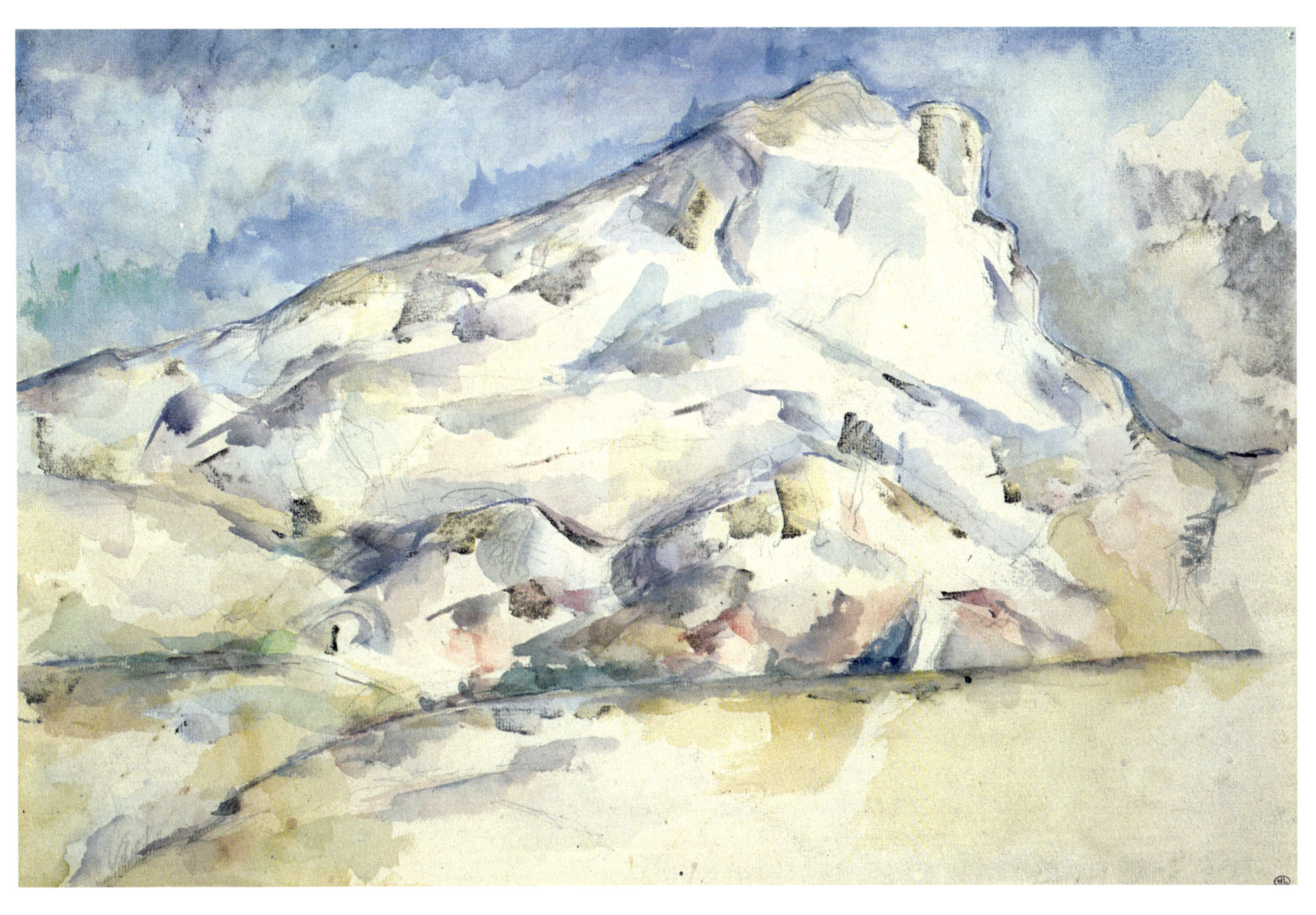

Fig. 5
La Montagne Sainte-Victoire, 1900–02 (probably earlier)
Graphite and watercolour on laid paper, 12⁷⁄₁₆ × 18¹⁵⁄₁₆ in. (31.6 × 48 cm)
Musée d'Orsay, held in the Musée du Louvre, département des arts
graphiques, Paris (RF31171)

Not far from there, he found a second subject which he repeatedly
tackled on paper from Vidalon and which is also included in this exhibition.
The sandstone cliffs above the château and in the adjacent quarry of
Bibémus form the subject of three half-sheets.[26] Cezanne captured one
rock formation twice on the same paper from different vantage points and
executed one of them in watercolour alone (cat.3, p.53).[27] Using the tip
of the brush as though it were a pencil, he traced the outline of the rock
formation and then filled it in with the brush held at a more acute angle.
Patches of vertical hatching accentuate the central rocks; short diagonals
and squiggles suggest the surrounding vegetation. With its well-preserved
luminosity of the pigments – rich in red and ochre set against shades of
green and blue – the palette recalls *Montagne Sainte-Victoire* and *Paysage
provençal* (cats 1 and 2, pp.49, 51). The fact that each of the sheets identified
so far on which Cezanne captured this particular rock formation is of the
same paper brand suggests that he engaged with the subject over a brief
period of time.[28]

Within the same watermark group, there is a third subject on which
the artist worked intensively within a limited span of time. There is a link
between the depictions of a single male figure wearing a hat and seated
at a table and the series of paintings of card players that Cezanne created
between the end of 1890 (probably with greater intensity from 1892)
and 1896 on the small farm that was part of the Jas de Bouffan estate.[29]
He produced a total of 11 single portraits of the card players on paper. Five
of these are on laid paper, all of it made in Vidalon.[30] Only two of them are
watercolours (one illustrated here, fig.6).[31] Their palette is similar to that
of the *Rochers près des grottes au-dessus de Château Noir* mentioned above (cat.3,
p.53), but with the addition of a significant amount of black in the depiction
of the figures, the contour lines and the background. As in that view too,
he worked without graphite, preferring instead to draw with the brush.

Until recently, no connection was made between these figure studies
and the landscapes. It was only the discovery of the shared paper support
that prompted reconsideration and suggested the inclusion of the remaining works on paper from Vidalon in a comparative study. This broadens
the range of subjects and motifs, adding individual trees, rocks in the
undergrowth, a bend in the road and an avenue, a still life, an imaginary
figurative scene and a sculpture of a cupid which in Cezanne's lifetime was
attributed to Pierre Puget (1620–1694) (fig.7).[32] Cezanne owned a plaster
cast of the sculpture – *L'Amour en plâtre* – which remained in his studio at
Les Lauves after his death.[33] Like the locatable landscape views, this figure

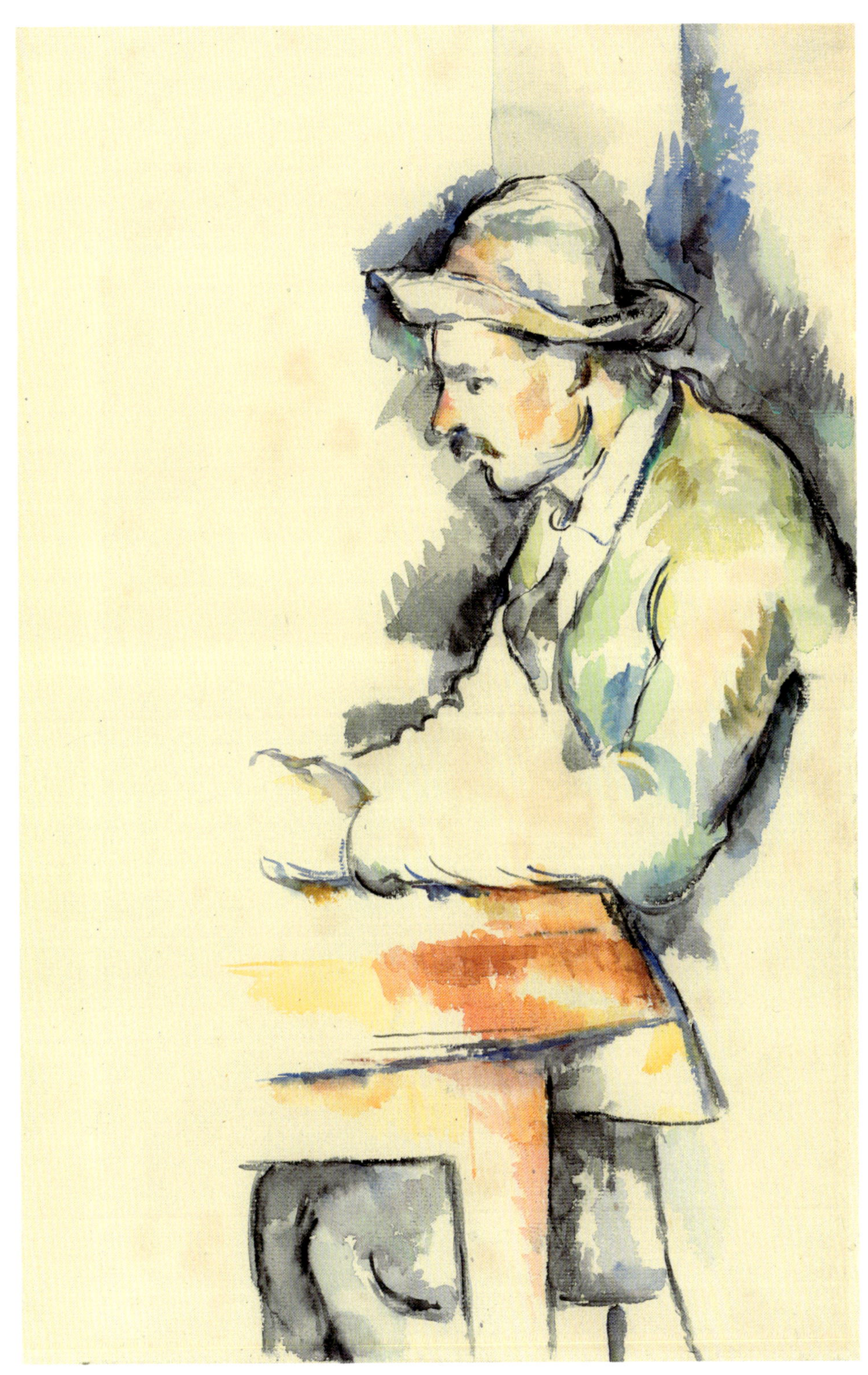

Fig.6
Joueur de cartes, 1892–96
Watercolour on laid paper, 18⅜ × 12 in. (46.7 × 30.5 cm)
Private collection

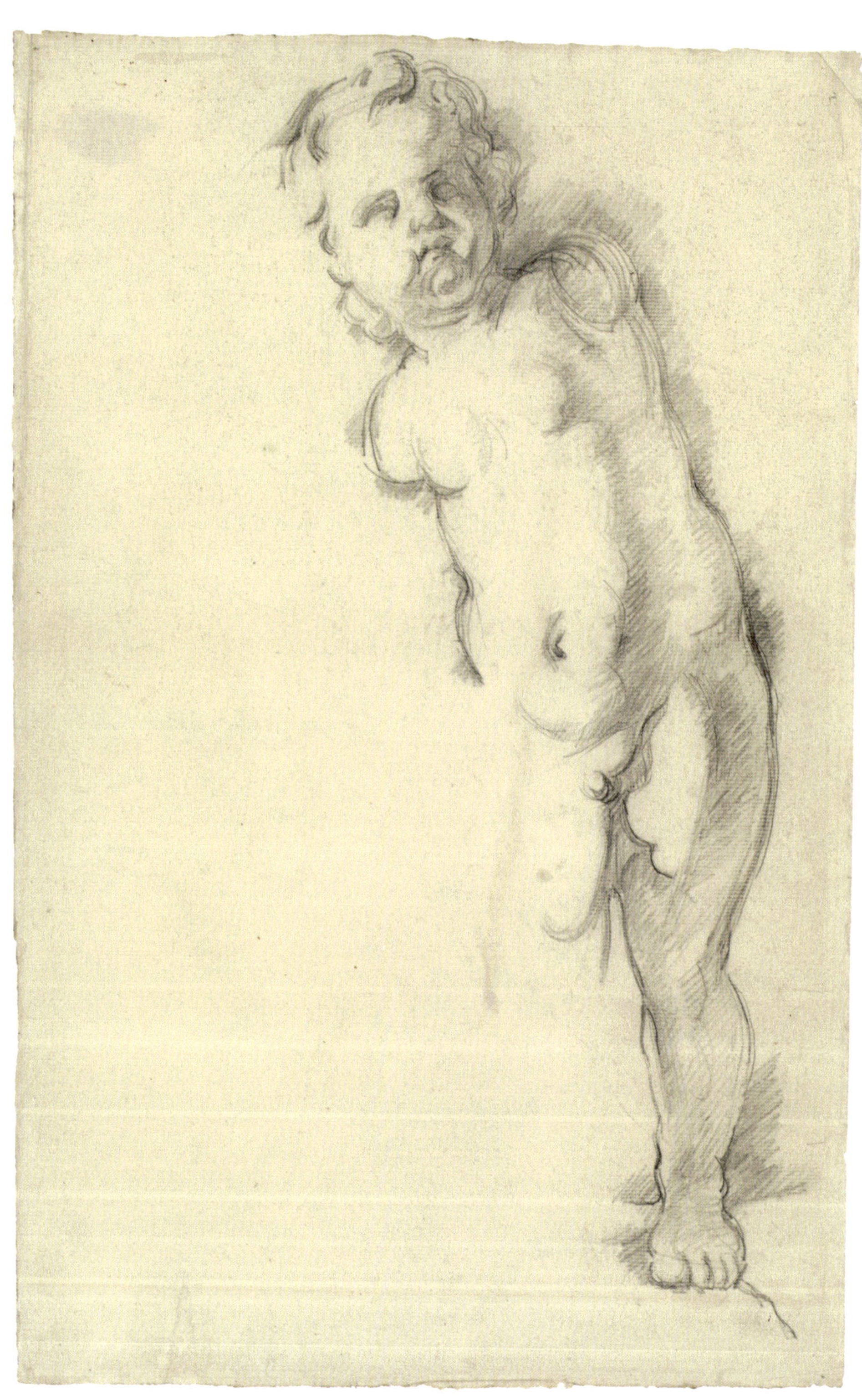

Fig.7
L'Amour en plâtre, c.1890
Graphite on laid paper, 19⁹⁄₁₆ × 12⁹⁄₁₆ in. (49.7 × 31.9 cm)
The British Museum, London

thus points to Aix and its surroundings as the area where papers with the 'VIDALON' or 'S A V' watermarks were used. This suggests that Cezanne executed the otherwise unlocatable studies of branches and rubble and the imaginary figure scene there as well. Dating of the individual sheets remains speculative, but Cezanne's use of the storage shed in the grounds of the Château Noir and the studies of the figures linked to the *Joueurs de cartes* suggest most of them were made between the late 1880s and mid-1890s.[34]

The palette shared by the watercolours of this group supports the assumption that they were created within a limited time span. Moreover, there are compositional parallels. To establish formal analogies between the posture of the seated man, the standing cupid and the gradient of the rock face may be a little far-fetched. But what we can observe within this watermark group, across the different genres, is the artist's interest in the spatial relations of bodies and objects, which he constructs as horizontal layers. This approach is most evident in the images of the rock formation. The composition of the one mentioned above is strikingly symmetrical (cf. cat.3, p.53). The arrangement of the visual elements is reminiscent of a tower, with the horizontally divided boulder in the centre perfectly balanced on two delicate saplings, which are rendered with feathery, slightly offsct strokes. More rocks are sitting on top, grouped, as if by chance, around the central vertical axis. The volume of the frontally shown plaster putto, captured in a frequent repetition of contour lines, is rendered in a similarly compact manner (cf. fig.7). By emphasising light and shadow – a patch of light on the left thigh, for example, is outlined so prominently that it resembles a flat ornament – Cezanne conveys the impression of a body made up of several separate components. The layering is distinctly less dense in a sparingly coloured drawing in the collection of the Musée Granet in Aix (cat.4, p.55).[35] Here, the spatial structure delineated in graphite has been made more prominent by the fading of the watercolour pigments, which have lost much of their former vibrancy. Trees and rocks are horizontally stacked on top of each other, suggesting that they are on the same plane. By contrast, the sweeping panoramic views of the complementing sheets depicting *Montagne Sainte-Victoire* and *Paysage provençal*, which are similarly divided into horizontal zones but have a clearly defined foreground, middle ground and background, convey a sense not so much of compression as of depth.

‘J V’

Cezanne's preoccupation with layering is also evident in a second group
of images in this exhibition, executed on a different make of laid paper.
And it is this similar focus that in a targeted comparison enables us to
identify approaches that are specific to certain watermark groups. This
second group also includes two panoramas. Not only do these views and the
Paysage provençal (discussed above) share certain characteristics in terms of
landscape, but compositional parallels among the works also suggest that
Cezanne was driven by similar interests, such as questions of how to create
pictorial depth.[36] But here Cezanne took a different approach. Compared
with the views on papers from Vidalon, he shifted the horizon upwards and
chose a slightly more narrowly framed view. In one half-sheet – now in a
private collection – he divided the panorama into three planes (cat.8, p.63).[37]
In the foreground, pushing in from the right, a concave spur of a hill reaches
into the centre of the composition, while on the left a convex arc stretches
into the middle ground, where it meets the corner and pitched roof of a
house. A plain behind extends to a mountain ridge, which Chappuis
identified as the Sainte-Baume, south-east of Aix. A few densely hatched
patches contrast strikingly with large expanses of untouched paper. These
contrasts of light and dark make the mountain range in the background
look like a band; shaded areas run through the plain and foreground and
suggest dark furrows. In the second panorama of this watermark group,
a drawing held by the Ashmolean Museum in Oxford, these tonal zones,
which Cezanne emphasised with forceful contour lines, are translated into
colour and thus look somewhat softened (cat.7, p.61).[38] Using graphite
sparingly, Cezanne sketched only the basic features of the landscape,
employing light hatch marks here and there, which only in some places
in the foreground come together as a tonal value. He went over this loose
structure with luminous watercolour pigments, which have since faded.
The colour connects the different planes of the image and imbues the
view with an airy lightness that is further heightened by the details in the
middle ground. A prominent house is echoed by a second, barely hinted at,
on the same spatial plane a little further to the right. Vegetation structures
the plain and extends onto the hill spur in the left foreground. Also titled
Paysage provençal, the view has the same balanced ratio of graphite and
watercolour as the panorama of the same name discussed earlier. But unlike
that image executed on a half-sheet with the ‘S A V’ monogram, both views
from the second watermark group feature more compact aggregations of

Fig.8
Detail of cat.7, *Paysage provençal*, 1885–90, showing the wire-formed watermark 'J V' in transmitted light

graphite and watercolour that form bands along contour lines.[39] However, like that of the papers marked 'S A V' or 'VIDALON', this group, also consists primarily of landscapes. Of the six sheets examined thus far, five are devoted to landscape: the aforementioned surroundings of Aix, an avenue at Jas de Bouffan, a single tree, and a view of grass, shrubs and trees by a low wall.[40] The shared support suggests that Cezanne found all these motifs in the same area.

The sixth sheet is markedly different in both subject matter and format. Instead of a landscape it shows three studies of individual male bathers, and it is a fragment rather than a half-sheet.[41] When the half-sheet was divided – it has not been possible to establish whether this was done by Cezanne himself or by a different hand – the watermark was divided as well, leaving only the lower half of the sans-serif letters 'J V'; on the five half-sheets, the letters are centrally placed (fig.8).[42] The paper historian Louis André has brought to my attention a laid paper used by an unidentified artist, on which 'J V' is the countermark corresponding to the 'PLANCH[ER BAS]' main mark.[43] This is significant since Cezanne purchased another make of paper from the mill owned by Émile Desloye in the town of Plancher-Bas (*département* Haute-Saône) in the Bourgogne-Franche-Comté region.[44] 'J V' could stand for an as yet unidentified customer of Desloye. Mills produced papers to order for retailers, specialist shops, publishers and artists and marked the different batches with client-specific watermarks.[45]

Cezanne used most of the papers that can securely be attributed to Desloye around 1885. The catalogue raisonnés date the works on 'J V' papers to around the same time, and thus a few years earlier than those on paper from Vidalon,[46] but there is no conclusive evidence to support these suggested dates. All the more valuable, then, is the fact that we have concrete information on the dates of creation of some works on 'J V' paper by a contemporary of Cezanne. Teio Meedendorp cites four examples of Vincent van Gogh (1853–1890) using paper with this watermark and suggests that it came from a 'watercolour block' fashioned by the artist himself in May 1883.[47] This lends some weight to the assumption that Cezanne used the same make of paper in the mid-1880s.[48]

The third make of paper shown in this exhibition was used later, and it is partly for this reason that the works differ from those on the two other brands in terms of subject and technique. No other watermark has been recorded as often as the line 'MONTGOLFIER | SAINT | MARCEL | LES | ANNONAY –' in serif letters (figs 9a and 9b). It refers to Saint-Marcel-lès-Annonay near Vidalon, where another branch of the Montgolfier family ran a paper mill.[49] The impressed watermark, which was applied in a continuous band along one of the edges of the damp paper with a narrow wheel called a *molette*, can be found on at least 42 of Cezanne's sheets.[50] According to the latest research, this watermark group is the largest and most homogeneous within Cezanne's work on paper. The artist used papers from Saint-Marcel almost exclusively for watercolours. The identified subjects demonstrate that while he executed a few of these in the grounds of the Château Noir, the majority were done in and around his studio at Les Lauves, and thus between 1902 and 1906.[51] The smooth texture of the relatively thick wove paper – comparable to that of a finely woven fabric – was ideally suited to the technique of Cezanne's late watercolours.[52]

This is exemplified in the exhibition by a landscape watercolour showing the view of the Saint-Sauveur cathedral in Aix with the l'Etoile mountain range in the background, seen from the terrace of Cezanne's studio (cat.5b, p.57).[53] The presence of multiple pinholes in each of the four corners attest to a drawn-out painting process that extended over several

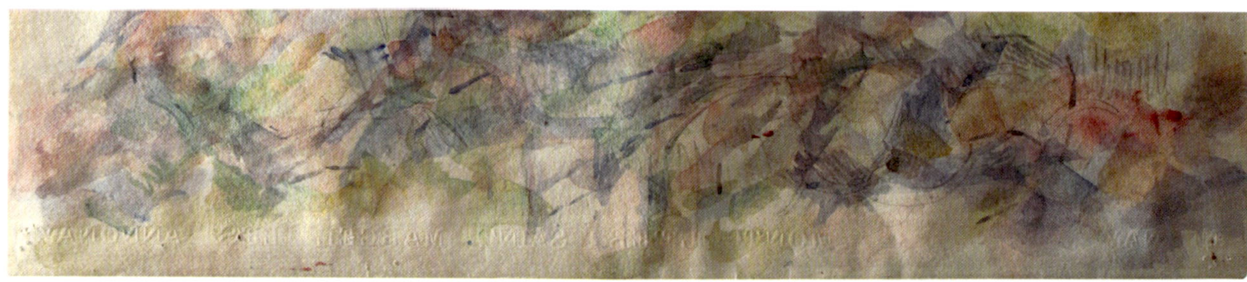

Figs 9a and 9b
Details of cat.6, *Route avec arbres sur une pente*, c.1904, showing parts of the impressed watermark 'MONTGOLFIER | SAINT | MARCEL | LES | ANNONAY –' in raking light
Top: recto (felt side of sheet); Bottom: verso (wire side of sheet)

sessions, during which Cezanne also turned the sheet over and sketched another landscape on the verso (cat.5a, p.56).[54] Long splashes of paint on the lower left corner of the recto suggest that at some stage he worked with the sheet upright, possibly on an easel. Over a loose sketch executed in a soft black pencil, he applied pink, lemon yellow and turquoise watercolour pigments in several, often overlapping layers.[55] The fact that these did not bleed into each other shows that he waited for each layer to dry before moving on to the next.[56] Heavily diluted, the pigments have a transparency that allows the beholder to follow Cezanne's distinctive layering of the composition. Layers applied early on shine through and converge with short strokes that are more dabbed than painted to create a shimmering tapestry of colour. Cezanne used the same broken contour lines, drawn with the point of his brush in viscous red or blue, to accentuate the spherical volumes of unidentifiable vegetation, as well as the tree trunks and the cathedral. Close to the left edge of the composition, where these lines define rising branches that are met by other branches reaching down from above, they resemble tongues of flame. These branches – reinforced by lush foliage descending from the upper edge – form a bracket that frames the composition. The mirror image-like similarity between the silhouettes of the upper and lower edge creates a sense of disorientation.

Focusing closely on the ground, a central tree trunk and its branches and crown, the watercolour *Route avec arbres sur une pente* on a half-sheet in the collection of the Fondation Beyeler in Basel does not pose that problem (cat.6, p.59).[57] The technique is comparable but marked by a more intense interplay between pencil and brush. Cezanne's extensive use of graphite hatching, some of it clearly above the layers of watercolour, accords the silvery grey-black of the pencil marks the role of an equivalent colour value.[58] Pencil and brush create an interwoven, equalising juxtaposition and superimposition of lines and planes that conflate foreground and background. This merging of planes as well as the close focus invite the viewer to immerse themselves in the dense vegetation on the right, from which emerge here a bit of a horizon line, there a series of curves and loops that form a spiralling column.

Although this melding of foreground and background recalls the abovementioned pictures of the Bibémus quarry walls on half-sheets from Vidalon, Cezanne's approach here is fundamentally different. Instead of presenting a landscape view as a coherent structure to be understood and revealed, he has dissolved this structure into light in the works on paper from Saint-Marcel. This by no means diminishes the cohesion of the individual elements. They present themselves as both dense and airy, enfolded in an *enveloppe* of piercing reflected rays that Cezanne sought to capture.[59]

A general preoccupation with light and brightness values can be observed in all works on paper from Saint-Marcel across all genres. A clear majority – 31 of a total of 45 sides – show landscapes. Apart from a single study of the abovementioned *L'Amour en plâtre*, the group also contains three portraits.[60] Two of these show a man with a straw hat sitting outside on a simple wooden chair, his left hand resting on a stick (fig.10).[61] On a half-sheet in the collection of the Art Institute of Chicago, the only things that make him stand out from his surroundings, which are handled in the same pigments, are contour lines and a few areas in his clothing where the paper is left blank. The fact that Cezanne omitted the seated figure's left foot, leaving an empty, gaping trouser leg, integrates the man even more closely into his setting.

If this portrait, like the view of the cathedral, was painted on the terrace at Les Lauves – as is generally assumed by scholars – then it is likely that Cezanne also executed the ten still lifes on paper from Saint-Marcel in the same studio.[62] Emphatically horizontal in structure, the composition of one of them, *Nature morte avec carafe, bouteille, et fruits* (fig.11, p.36) in the collection of the Pearlman Foundation, New York, recalls that of *Vue sur Aix* (cat.5b, p.37).[63] The cognac bottle echoes the cathedral spire and constitutes the vertical counterpoint. Not only does the neck of the bottle coincide with the central vertical axis, the bottle also forms the heart of the composition in terms of colour. Countless layers of watercolour create an almost opaque colour field, whose darkness is intensified by the blank white space of the label. The translucent forms of the carafe, a glass that is barely hinted at and the panelling in the background stand in stark contrast to these dark hues.

The white surface of the paper plays an important role in these later watercolours. On the one hand it acts as a subtle but omnipresent brightness value; on the other, the bare ground serves as a colour value in its own right, as in the label of the bottle. Another example of the latter function is seen in a still life in the collection of the Art Institute of Chicago that shows three skulls on a table draped with a floral cloth (fig.12, p.39).[64] It is one of ten watercolours executed on a full sheet from Saint-Marcel. No other make of paper was used as often in this size. The full *raisin* format is similar to that of the standard canvas format of a *toile de 15 (figure)*, (65 by 54 centimetres), which he used for a thematically and chromatically closely related oil painting in the collection of the Kunstmuseum Solothurn.[65] Although it is

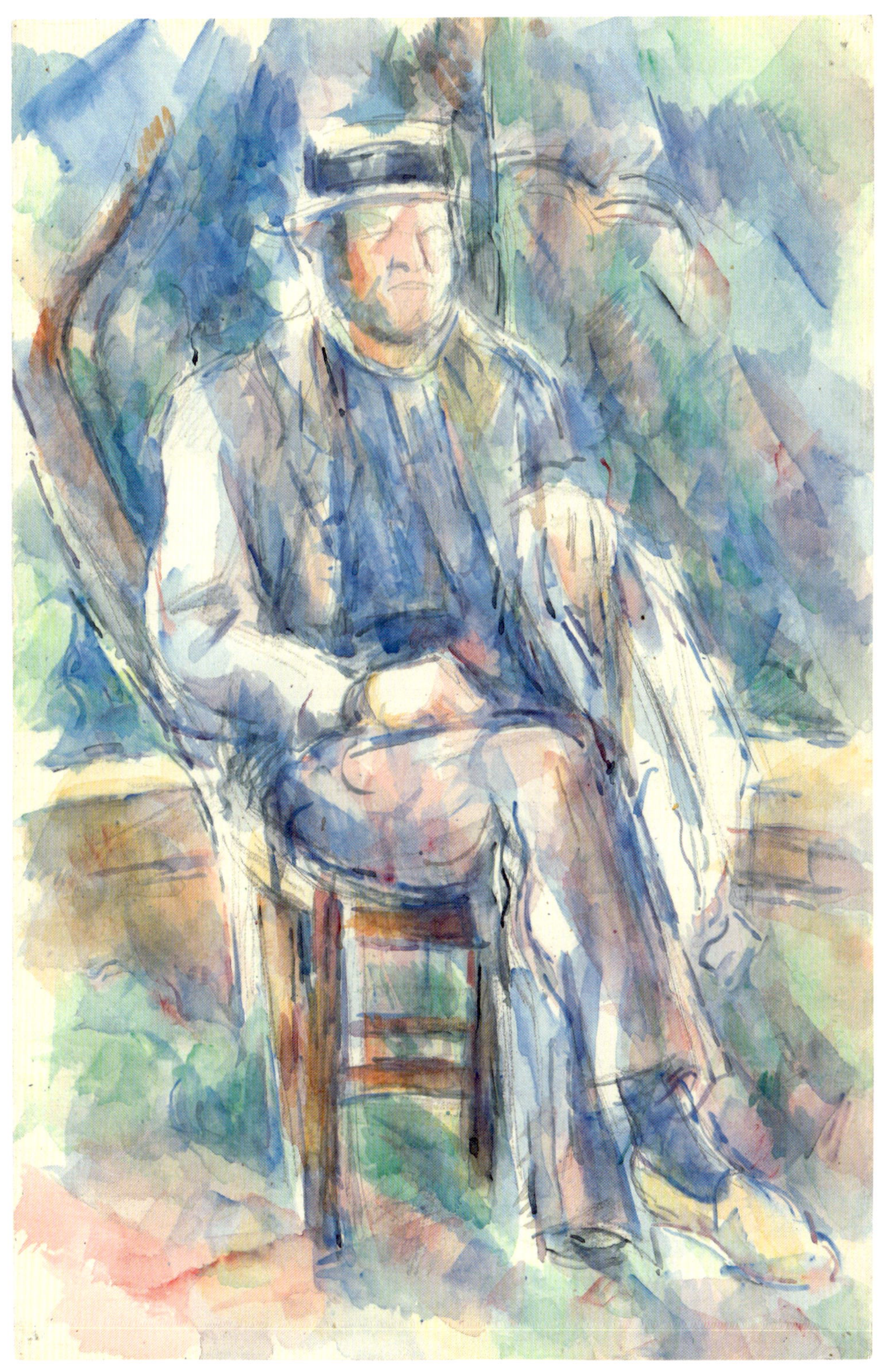

Fig.10
Paysan au canotier, c.1906
Graphite and watercolour on wove paper, 18⅞ × 12⅜ in. (47.9 × 31.5 cm)
The Art Institute of Chicago (Gift of Janis H. Palmer in memory of
Pauline K. Palmer)

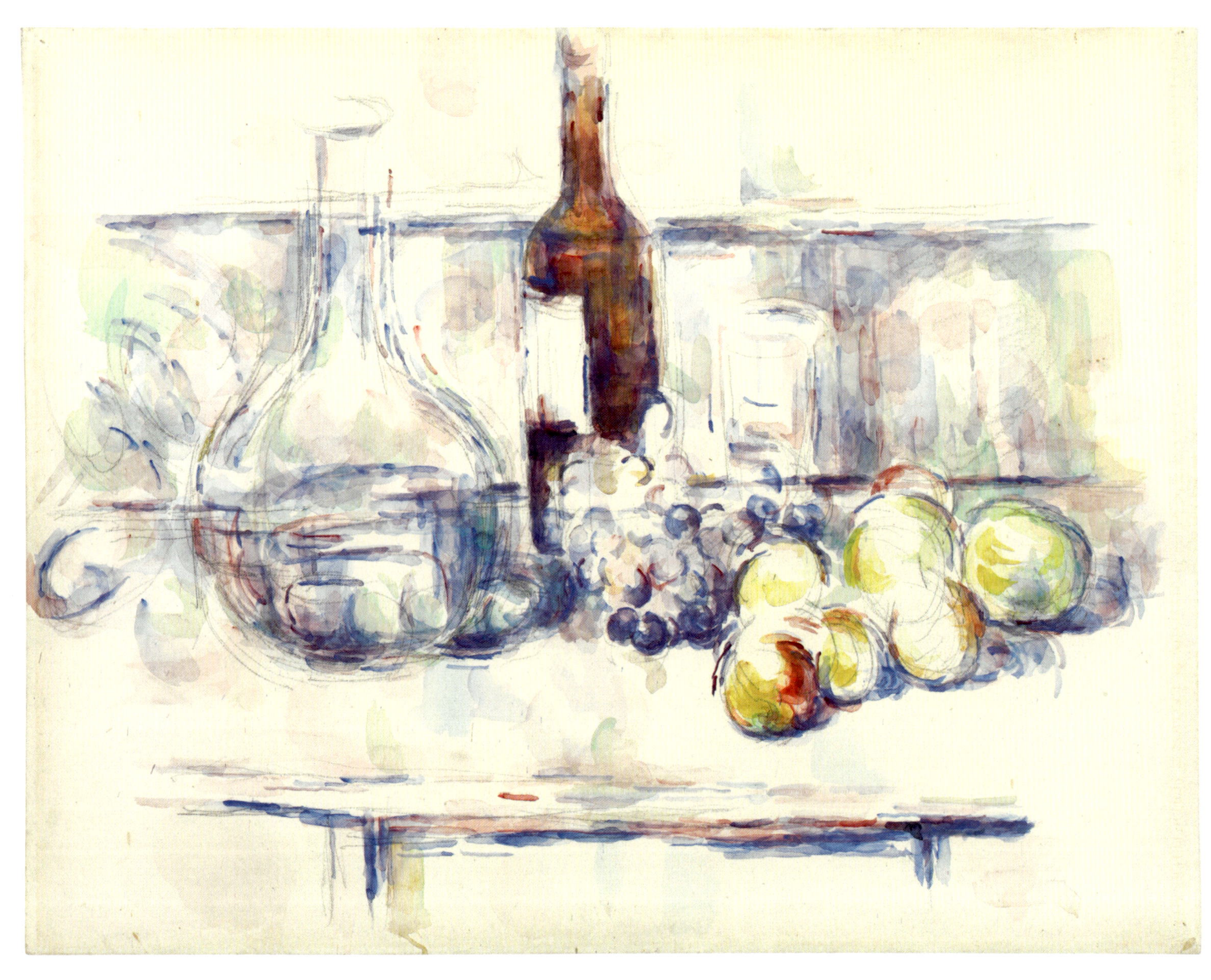

Fig.11
Nature morte avec carafe, bouteille, et fruits, 1906
Graphite and watercolour on wove paper, 19 × 24⁷⁄₁₆ in. (47 × 62 cm)
Henry and Rose Pearlman Foundation, New York
(on extended loan to the Princeton Art Museum)

36

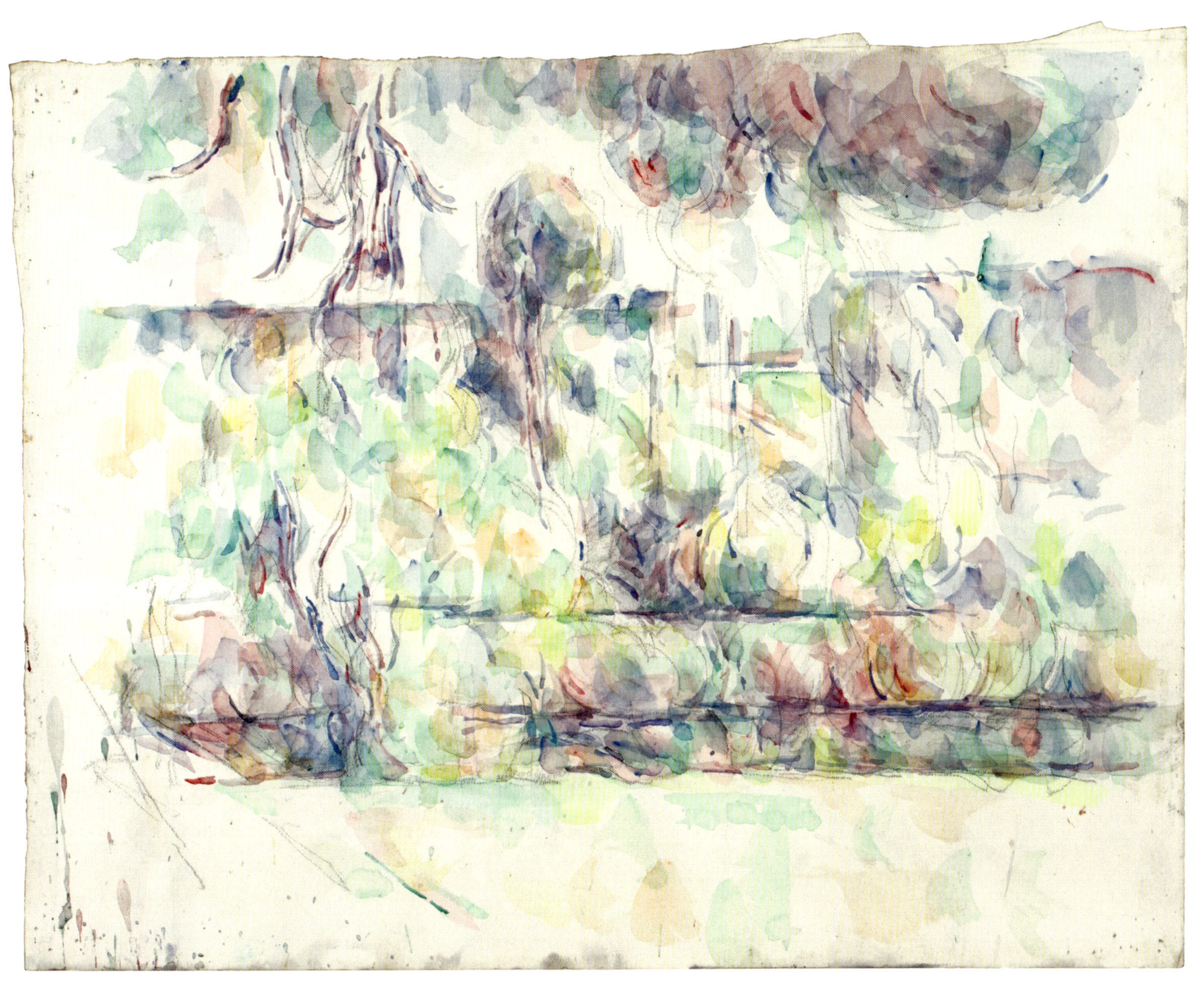

Cat.5b
Paul Cezanne (1839–1906)
Le Jardin des Lauves: vue sur Aix et la Cathédrale de Saint-Sauveur, 1902–06
Graphite and watercolour on wove paper, 15¾ × 22 in. (40 × 54 cm)
Private collection

safe to assume that Cezanne always worked on paper and canvas in parallel, finding inspiration in one medium for his work in the other, there are few examples in which this dialogue between the different media is as evident as in the still lifes of skulls. However, a comparison between the water-colour from Chicago and the oil painting from Solothurn demonstrates that similar effects require fundamentally different painterly processes. Working on canvas, Cezanne did not leave the skulls blank but assigned them the lightest shades in his palette, applying the paint in as many layers and with the same impasto as in the areas around them.[66] In watercolours such as *Bouteille, carafe, cruche et citrons* in the collection of the Museo Nacional Thyssen-Bornemisza (fig.1, p.13), which is also part of the Saint-Marcel watermark group, he consolidated the two techniques by not only omitting the surface of a centrally placed floral earthenware jug but accentuating it with white gouache.[67]

Traces of Immediacy

There are only very few eyewitness accounts or photographs that convey any sense of Cezanne's working methods.[68] His heavily reworked oil paintings have long intrigued art historians and prompted research into his technique.[69] Detailed technical analyses have contributed to a better understanding of his materials and of the composition and properties of his drawings, watercolours and oil paintings.[70] However, numerous ques-tions regarding the wider context of Cezanne's studio practice remain unanswered. We still do not know, for example, which compositions he created simultaneously or in rapid succession.

Apart from the Montagne Sainte-Victoire, there are several other sub-jects that Cezanne returned to time and again. These include groups of portraits (for example of his wife, Hortense Fiquet, and his son, Paul Cezanne *fils*), bathers in various constellations and carefully arranged still lifes that were created over the course of years or even decades. Looked at in isolation, each of these genres has formed the starting point for several exhibitions and a great deal of scholarly research. This has resulted in a subject-oriented, arbitrary division of Cezanne's oeuvre that hardly reflects the artist's complex creative process. The works on paper in particular illustrate the fluid transitions between disciplines and genres: working on small sketchbook pages and large-format loose sheets, Cezanne often produced several drawings on the same sheet, either in graphite or

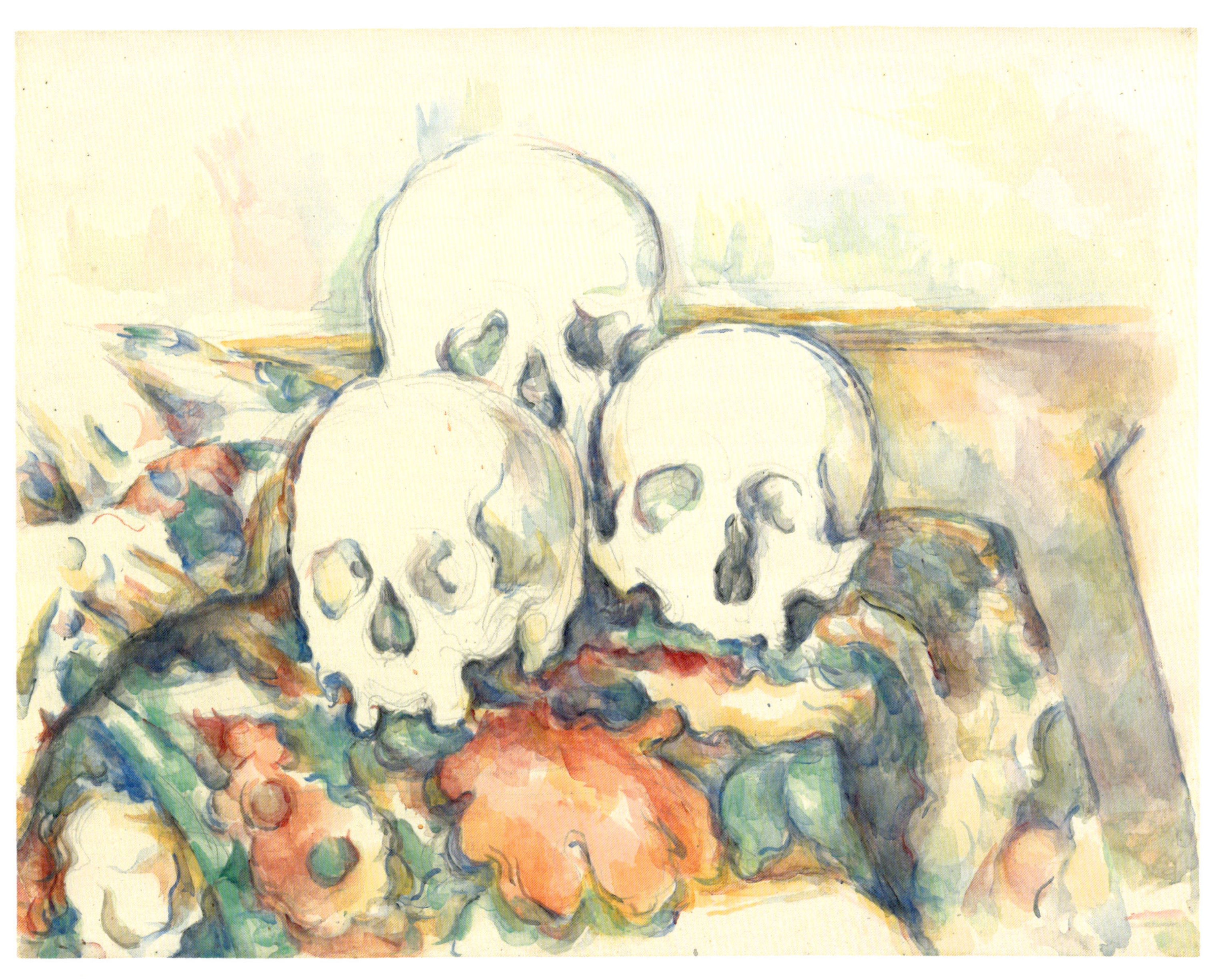

Fig.12
Trois crânes, 1902–06
Graphite and watercolour, touches of gouache on wove paper,
18⅞ × 24¾ in. (48 × 62.8 cm)
The Art Institute of Chicago (Olivia Shaler Swan Memorial Collection)

watercolour, or in a combination of the two media. Branches and limbs, heads and ginger jars appear on successive sketchbook pages, on the recto and verso of the same sheet, or even side by side or one on top of the other on the same page or sheet. For a better understanding of the artist's work, it is thus imperative to consider these proximities. If we conceive of the material context as a whole, then we can use these groups of works as starting points to ask which questions preoccupied Cezanne during a given period and how he tackled them in parallel in different media and genres.

While individual sketchbooks by Cezanne have already been fruitfully analysed as units, we previously lacked the tools to do this for the loose sheets.[71] Despite pioneering studies such as the one by Peter Bower on the paper used by J.M.W. Turner (1775–1851), watermarks continue to play a niche role in studies of nineteenth-century art.[72] However, as the focus on these three watermark groups within Cezanne's work demonstrates, closer consideration of paper qualities holds the promise of important discoveries – even for works produced in the nineteenth and early twentieth centuries, when artists could select from among a hitherto unimaginable range of papers. The contextualisation of 'individual' sheets can reveal previously overlooked links between works and help uncover potential chronological sequences – especially invaluable for an artist like Cezanne, who rarely dated any of his works. Moreover, the discovery of unexpected juxtapositions, based on the material of the support, may also help us to fundamentally reconsider works on paper by his contemporaries.

Art historians, collectors and museum visitors alike value drawings as an artist's most intimate kind of work. Ever since the Renaissance, sketches have been celebrated as ideas made manifest; the line on paper allows the beholder to share in an artist's train of thought.[73] This immediacy of content is echoed by the perception of the medium: particularly in the case of dry drawing materials, where it is the artist who holds the graphite pencil, charcoal or chalk, the marks thus created suggest a more direct encounter with the artist's hand than those made with an intermediary tool like a brush. On a third, material level, works on paper, by dint of the quality and condition of the support, provide additional intimate insights into an artist's creative practice and help to understand it in all its complexity.

NOTES

1 FWN 1167 (RW 279). For a detailed description of this work and an infrared reflectogram that clearly shows the graphite sketch, see Stephanie Buck, 'La Montagne Sainte-Victoire', in Buck, House, Vegelin van Claerbergen and Wright 2008, no.14, pp.120–23. Here and in the following, Cezanne's works are referred to by the numbers used in the online catalogue raisonné compiled under the direction of Walter Feilchenfeldt, Jayne Warman and David Nash (Feilchenfeldt, Warman and Nash 2014), preceded by the abbreviation FWN. Additionally, for paintings and watercolours the numbers are given for John Rewald's printed catalogue raisonné (Rewald 1996; Rewald 1983), abbreviated R or RW. The references for drawings are based on the entries in Adrien Chappuis' catalogue raisonné (Chappuis 1973), abbreviated Ch.

2 On the potential of such traces for the reconstruction of the biography of an object, see for example Motz 2019.

3 FWN 1155 (RW 243).

4 The author first published this discovery in Ruppen 2017c, pp.96–98. There are, however, several cases in which it was possible to reunite irregular fragments.

5 See Rewald 1983, no. 243.

6 On the people responsible for the fragmentation of Cezanne's oeuvre on paper and their possible motives, see Ruppen 2018, pp.43–83.

7 Innis Howe Shoemaker's reconstruction of the two so-called *Philadelphia Sketchbooks* in the collection of the Philadelphia Museum of Art is exemplary. Conspicuous pinholes allowed Shoemaker to identify numerous sheets that had been removed from one of the two sketchbooks; see Shoemaker 1989. See also the reconstruction of sketchbooks in the collection of the Kupferstichkabinett of the Kunstmuseum Basel, where a prominent stain attributed to an oil-based medium and rust from an old wire staple stitching provided decisive clues; Seger 2017. For a partial reconstruction of all known sketchbooks of Cezanne, see Ruppen 2018, pp.126–78.

8 On a selection of these everyday papers and their potential for the analysis of the works executed on them, see Ruppen 2017b, pp.223–25. For a discussion of the entire group, see Ruppen 2018, pp.103–25.

9 The author first formulated this observation in Ruppen 2017b, p.221. Apart from half-sheets, but in much smaller numbers, there are quarter- and eighth-sheets, probably cut by Cezanne himself. The numerous irregular fragments, however, are probably the result of interventions by early art dealers, see *ibid*. Ruppen 2017b, p.221; Ruppen 2018, pp.43–83.

10 For introductions to paper manufacturing, see, for example, Hunter 1957; Gaskell 1972; Loeber 1982; Tschudin 2007; Baker 2010.

11 The meanings denoted by watermarks differed from one location to another and changed frequently over the course of the centuries. The standard compendium for French seventeenth- and eighteenth-century watermarks is Gaudriault 1995; for French watermarks of the nineteenth century, see André 2011.

12 See a 1904 product catalogue of the specialist dealer Sennelier in Paris, which lists single *raisin*-format sheets of Canson white drawing paper for 0.15 francs, and sheets *à la main* for 2.75 francs: Sennelier 1904, 97, no. 1480. For a general introduction to nineteenth-century drawing materials, see Schenck 2005. Dealers would also offer drawing paper as sketchbooks or blocks and pads. However, only a handful of Cezanne's half-sheets show traces such as regular tears or remnants of glue, pointing to a block or pad origin. Furthermore, his known sketchbooks measure between 11.2 × 6.8 cm and 21.2 × 27.5 cm and are thus significantly smaller than his half-sheets of loose drawing paper.

13 Seurat worked almost exclusively on quarter-sheets of a laid paper watermarked 'MICHALLET'. For a detailed study see Buchberg 2007. Cezanne, too, repeatedly chose to work on that paper.

14 So far we know of only one sketchbook sheet by Cezanne that bears a

watermark; see fol. 32 in sketchbook Inv. 1999.9 in the collection of the Morgan Library and Museum, New York. On this watermark see Shelley 2014, pp.181–82, n. 32.

15   FWN 1118 (RW 170).

16   FWN 1365 (RW 423).

17   Although not all sheets of drawing paper are watermarked, the examination of the remaining 700 works is likely to lead to the discovery of numerous further watermarks.

18   Wire-formed watermarks, like the ribbed texture of handmade laid paper, are created by a form, usually made of wire, attached to the sieve. The wires displace the wet fibre mass, making the paper fractionally thinner and thus more translucent so that the pattern of the sieve and the watermark can be seen in transmitted light. With the introduction of machine-made paper, wire-formed watermarks were no longer applied in the sieve but with a dandy roll. See Zender 2008, p.292.

19   On countermarks, see Gaudriault 1995, p.28. Countermarks often consist of the initials of the mill's owner. Since not all watermarks have countermarks, many of Cezanne's works on half-sheets lack a watermark. Unless these sheets have other distinguishing marks – a characteristic texture, for example – they can only very rarely be assigned to a specific watermark group without additional technical study. If present, the main mark and countermark are often found individually on the separate halves of a sheet.

20   On Canson et Montgolfier, see the publications by Marie-Hélène Reynaud, for example Reynaud 1989.

21   See the paper sample catalogue of the Ancienne Manufacture Canson et Montgolfier, Carnet No 1. Papiers pur chiffon, Vidalon-lès-Annonay 1913. Listed under category VI are 'Papiers Ingres pour pastel & crayon. Marque: Monogramme SAV & "VIDALON".' As André explains, the introduction of commercial brands also gave rise to subtle hierarchies within the products of a paper mill; André 2011, p.93. According to another Canson et Montgolfier product catalogue, sheets marked 'VIDALON'/'SAV' were second-class papers ('pâte B') with a higher wood content than first-class paper ('pâte A') and therefore may deteriorate and discolour more quickly; Ancienne Manufacture Canson et Montgolfier, Prix courant des papiers en rouleaux et en rames de la Société Anonyme des Papeteries de Vidalon, Vidalon-lès-Annonay 1888. Both catalogues are preserved in the Archives du Musée des Papeteries Canson et Montgolfier, Vidalon. The author is grateful to Marie-Hélène Reynaud for granting her access to the holdings of the archive.

22   See Reynaud 1989, p.84.

23   The Société Anonyme des Papeteries de Vidalon was founded on 27 December 1880; see Reynaud 1989, p.103. The author thanks Marie-Hélène Reynaud for her assessment that an occasional earlier use of the 'S A V' watermark cannot be ruled out.

24   The author first discussed this watermark group in Ruppen 2017c, pp.92–98. For a list of all the works identified then, see *ibid.*, p.99, n.31. Since then the 'VIDALON' watermark has been found on two further half-sheets; see FWN 1388 (RW 432) and FWN 1524.

25   FWN 1442 (RW 496) and FWN 1447 (RW 504) are held by the Barnes Foundation; FWN 1458 (RW 502) is in the collection of the Musée d'Orsay. For a detailed comparison of these three views of the Montagne Sainte-Victoire based on their supports, see the author's entry in the catalogue of works by Cezanne in the collection of the Barnes Foundation (forthcoming, 2020).

26   For the view of the *Rochers à Bibémus*, see FWN 1232 (RW 306); for the two views of the *Rochers près des grottes au-dessus de Château Noir*, see FWN 1388 (RW 432) and FWN 1391 (RW 434). In a drawing on a half-sheet with the 'VIDALON' watermark that entered the collection of the Kunstmuseum Bern in 2014 as part of the Gurlitt Bequest, Cezanne captured the so-called Maison Maria, a building in the grounds of the Château Noir; FWN 1524. The drawing, which was included in the online catalogue raisonné in the summer of 2019, is closely related to the painting FWN 309 (R 792) at the Kimbell Art Museum, Fort Worth. For a photograph of the motif, see Rewald and Marschutz 1935, p.16, fig.4.

27   FWN 1388 (RW 432).

28   It remains to be ascertained whether any of the remaining four pictures of the rock face were executed on 'S A V'/'VIDALON' paper. One of these four half-sheets is a piece of wove paper also made in Vidalon; FWN 1390 (RW 435). Two are sheets of laid papers that have not yet been examined for watermarks; FWN 1389 (RW 433) and FWN 1394 (RW 439). The image of the fourth half-sheet does not allow for an identification; FWN 1392 (RW 438).

29   On Cezanne's *Joueurs de cartes*, see Ireson and Wright 2010.

30   They are FWN 1762 (Ch 1094), FWN 1763 (RW 380), FWN 1765 (Ch 1092) and FWN 1766 (Ch 1095)/ FWN 1767 (RW 378). Cezanne executed FWN 1758 (Ch 1061), FWN 1759 (RW 381), FWN 1760 (RW 377), FWN 1761 (RW 379) and FWN 1764 (Ch 1093) on loose wove paper sheets; FWN 3002-43b (Ch 439) on a sketchbook page. Also executed on a loose sheet of wove paper is a further closely related portrait of a man wearing a hat who does not, however, appear in any of the known paintings and is therefore not considered to belong to the *Joueurs de cartes* group; FWN 1777 (RW 542).

31   FWN 1763 (RW 380), FWN 1767 (RW 378).

32   FWN 2162 (Ch 988).

33   For an image of the plaster cast, see Berthold 1958, fig.10. For a discussion of the sculpture see Reff 1960, p.147, n.16.

34   There are several slightly different versions of both watermarks on the papers used by Cezanne. Transmitted light images, which would enable us to divide the watermarks into subgroups and thus date them more precisely, are currently only available for some of them

35   FWN 1524.

36   Rewald already observed similarities between the two landscapes FWN 1206 (RW 262) and FWN 1155 (RW 243); see Rewald 1983, no.243.

37   FWN 1133 (Ch 899).

38 FWN 1206 (RW 262).

39 This is particularly striking in a view
of the avenue at Jas de Bouffan in
the collection of the Boijmans van
Beuningen Museum in Rotterdam,
which also forms part of this second
watermark group. See FWN 1164
(Ch 916).

40 See FWN 1217 (Ch 927) and FWN 1190
(Ch 1185). Furthermore, Jon Whiteley
recorded 'faint traces of a view with
a viaduct and a tree on the right' on
the verso of FWN 1206 (RW 262). He
identified those traces as an offset of the
watercolour *Pin devant la vallée de l'Arc*,
held in the Albertina, Vienna (FWN 1129
[RW 239]), and thus reckons that the
Oxford watercolour is contemporary
and was drawn nearby; Whiteley
2000, no.987. The watercolour in the
Albertina was executed on a half-sheet
of laid paper that is mounted and therefore cannot be checked for a watermark.
However, the offset suggests that it is
part of the same group.

41 FWN 2038 (Ch 946). Measuring
22.7 × 29.5 cm, this sheet is slightly
smaller than a quarter-sheet.

42 For an image of the fragmented watermark, see Haldemann 2017, p.275, no.7.

43 Email from Louis André to the author,
10 February 2018. According to André,
the drawing bears the date 1869. The
serif font distinguishes this watermark
from the 'J V' examples in Cezanne's
work.

44 The main mark on these sheets of
laid paper reads 'PL BAS', and the
countermarks are either 'E D C' or
'E D & Cie' in a cartouche. For an
examination of this watermark group
see Ruppen 2019.

45 See André 2011, p.89.

46 Chappuis dates Ch 899 to 1883–86,
Ch 916 to 1884–87, Ch 927 to 1886–89,
Ch 946 to 1886–89 and Ch 1185 to
1900–04. Rewald dates RW 262 to
1885–90, Venturi dates it to 1885–86; see
Venturi 1936, no.910.

47 See Meedendorp 2007, p.204, n.2.
For a transmitted light image of the
watermark, see *ibid.*, p.429, fig.10.

48 Van Gogh captured a potato field
behind dunes in ink and gouache on
a pink-brown fragment of 'J V' paper;
see Meedendorp 2007, pp.203–05.

While Cezanne's 'J V' papers bear no
trace of ever having had a pink tint,
the 'J V' watermark illustrated by
Meedendorp is in a sans-serif font and
similar to one of three slightly different
versions of the watermark that could
be documented in Cezanne's work.
The stem of the 'J' and the up- and
downstrokes of the 'V' are of the same
width; the feet of both letters rest on
the same laid line. This first version
can be found on the two half-sheets
FWN 1164 (Ch 916) and FWN 1190
(Ch 1185) as well as on the fragment
FWN 2038 (Ch 946). A second, slightly
different version can be found on the
half-sheets FWN 1206 (RW 262) and
FWN 1217 (Ch 927). So far FWN 1133
(Ch 899) is the only half-sheet
representing a third version.

49 Of the three Montgolfier mills the
one in Vidalon-lès-Annonay is the
oldest. After the death of Étienne de
Montgolfier in 1799, his son-in-law
Barthélémy Barou de Canson took over
the mill, which was renamed Canson
et Montgolfier in 1801. Étienne de
Montgolfier's nephew, Jean-Baptiste
de Montgolfier, built a mill in Saint-
Marcel that started production in 1805.
In 1853 the sons of Jean-Baptiste
de Montgolfier divided it into two
businesses, Montgolfier in Saint-Marcel
and Montgolfier Frères in Grosberty.
On the history of the mills and the
Montgolfier family, see Reynaud 1989,
especially pp.102, 104. For a family tree,
see *ibid.*, pp.106–07.

50 Impressed watermarks are made by
running a narrow wheel called a *molette*
on the damp paper after it has left
the wire section. In contrast to wire-
formed watermarks, the paper is not
thinned but compressed. Impressed
watermarks are best studied under
raking light, which shows them as
reliefs. See Zender 2008, p.292. On
some of Cezanne's sheets the sequence
of words 'MONTGOLFIER | SAINT
| MARCEL | LES | ANNONAY –' runs
along the long side of the sheet, on
others along the short side. Because it is
a continuous sequence, the location of
the interruption in the latter provides
a clue to matching half-sheets.

51 For three views of the Château Noir

or a pistachio tree in its courtyard,
see FWN 1322 (RW 394), FWN 1449
(RW 515) and FWN 1450 (RW 516).

52 Faith Zieske's analysis of Cezanne's
papers in the collection of the
Philadelphia Museum of Art has shown
that two sheets from Saint-Marcel
were significantly thicker than other
wove papers used by Cezanne in the
same collection (0.28 mm as opposed
to merely 0.20–0.21 mm). They are also
considerably more hard-wearing than
a laid paper sheet with a 'VIDALON'
watermark in the same collection that
measures only 0.17 mm; see Zieske
2002, p.96, table 2.5. The two sheets
from Saint-Marcel, which Zieske
examined, are made of rags alone.
The fact that the paper is still a brilliant
white is probably at least partly due to
the high quality of the fibres; see *ibid.*,
p.98.

53 FWN 1486 (RW 622).

54 FWN 1487.

55 Rewald defined this palette in
combination with a 'cumulative'
colour application as typical of the
watercolours produced at Les Lauves
and its surroundings; see Rewald 1983,
no.611.

56 On this, see Zieske 2002, p.90. The
narrow accumulations of more highly
concentrated colour along the edges
of the strokes also bears witness to this
method.

57 FWN 1509 (RW 625).

58 In recent years, several authors have
stressed the close relationship between
graphite and watercolour in Cezanne's
works on paper. See especially Carol
Armstrong, who speaks of a 'dialogic
relation between graphite lines and
watercolor veils', and Matthew Simms,
who accurately describes Cezanne's
watercolours as a 'hybrid medium',
'between drawing and painting';
Armstrong 2004, p.108; Simms 2008,
p.199.

59 Paul Cezanne, letter to Émile Bernard,
1905: 'Dessinez; mais c'est le reflet qui
est enveloppant, la lumière, par le reflet
général, c'est l'enveloppe' (Draw, but
remember: the play of light defines
the object, light contains all). Cited
in Rewald 1937, pp.275–76, here 276;
translation in Rewald 1984, pp.310–11,

here 311. Geneviève Monnier accurately spoke of a 'kaleidoscopic effect': '[H]e [Cezanne, F. R.] seems to be striving to achieve a double purpose: the isolation of certain planes observed in detail and also the representation of a nature constantly moving in accord with the vibrations of light and its reflections, in a new vision that might be called "kaleidoscopic".' Monnier 1977, p.114.

60 For the picture of the *Amour en plâtre*, see FWN 2180 (RW 556); for the three portraits, see FWN 1757 (RW 383), FWN 1780 (RW 639) as well as FWN 1779 (RW 638), discussed in what follows.

61 FWN 1779 (RW 638); FWN 1780 (RW 639).

62 These still lifes are FWN 1959 (RW 544), FWN 1961 (RW 546), FWN 1967 (RW 563), FWN 1969 (RW 552), FWN 1970 (RW 572), FWN 1972 (RW 562), FWN 1978 (RW 567), FWN 1985 (RW 613), FWN 1987 (RW 611) and FWN 1988 (RW 642).

63 FWN 1988 (RW 642).

64 FWN 1987 (RW 611).

65 FWN 875 (R 824). For a list of French canvas formats and their use by Cezanne, see Feilchenfeldt 1996, p.16.

66 The aforementioned portrait of the *Paysan* in the collection of the Art Institute of Chicago and a closely related painting in the collection of the Museo Nacional Thyssen-Bornemisza in Madrid represent a different strategy. The watercolour does not have a single local highlight; instead, the paper surface shines through at several carefully chosen places. This effect is replicated in the painting, where small areas of the blank primed canvas are visible. Whereas the translucent watercolour lets the white paper shimmer through even in places where it has been applied in several layers, the primed canvas is visible only in those places where Cezanne left a gap in the layers of opaque oil paint. See FWN 546 (R 952) and FWN 1779 (RW 638). Comparable in approach are a portrait of his gardener Vallier on a half-sheet from Saint-Marcel, FWN 1780 (RW 639), and two closely related paintings, FWN 547 (R 950) and FWN 548 (R 953). See John Elderfield, 'Outdoor Portraits of Vallier, the Gardener', in Elderfield 2017, pp.211–17.

67 FWN 1967 (RW 614).

68 For descriptions of Cezanne's working methods by his contemporaries, see for example Émile Bernard's recollections of visits to Cezanne in 1904 and 1905, 'Souvenirs sur Paul Cézanne et lettres inédites', published in two instalments on 1 and 16 October 1907 in the *Mercure de France*. As Michael Doran has pointed out, Bernard's 'recollections' provide important clues in relation to Cezanne's painting technique but need to be taken with a grain of salt; see Doran 1978, p.49.

69 The first comprehensive study of this subject is Robert Ratcliffe's unpublished PhD dissertation 'Cézanne's Working Methods and their Theoretical Background', submitted to the Courtauld Institute in 1960; see Ratcliffe 1960.

70 On Cezanne's paintings, see for example Butler 1994; Reissner 2008a; Reissner 2008b; Burnstock, Hale, Campbell and Macaro 2010; Hale 2014. On his watercolours, see Zieske 2002; Reissner 2008b. On the drawings, see Shelley 2014; Seger 2017.

71 For analyses of sketchbook units, see especially Rewald 1951; Schniewind 1951; Andersen 1962; Andersen 1965; Chappuis 1966; Rewald 1982; Reff and Shoemaker 1989; Ruppen 2017a; Ruppen 2018, pp.126–78.

72 See Bower 1990; Bower 1999. Bower examined Turner's papers and used their watermarks to reconstruct fragmented sheets. The fact that art historians have largely disregarded nineteenth-century French watermarks until now may be due to the wide range of available papers and the paucity of surviving paper mill archives; see Ruppen 2019.

73 On the change in the concepts of *disegno* and *idea*, which occurred in the sixteenth century, see for example Kemp 1974.

AUTHOR'S NOTE

This essay is based on my PhD thesis, 'Der fragmentierte Cézanne. Zur Rekonstruktion von Skizzenbüchern und losen Blättern', supervised by Wolfgang Kersten and Bettina Gockel, with Richard Shiff as external adviser and submitted at the Institute of Art History at the University of Zurich in July 2018. The research project received generous support from a great many people. With regard to the present essay, I would especially like to thank Louis André, Marian Dirda (Paper Sample Archive at the National Gallery of Art, Washington DC) and Marie-Hélène Reynaud (director of the Musée des Papeteries Canson et Montgolfier in Vidalon, Davézieux) for sharing their knowledge and understanding of paper qualities and watermarks. I am grateful to Sophie Junge for reviewing my manuscript and to Sophie Kullmann for critical remarks.

Exhibited Works

Cat.1
Paul Cezanne (1839–1906)
La Montagne Sainte-Victoire, 1885–87
Graphite and watercolour on laid paper, 12⅞ × 19⅞ in. (32.7 × 50.5 cm)
The Courtauld Gallery, London (The Samuel Courtauld Trust)

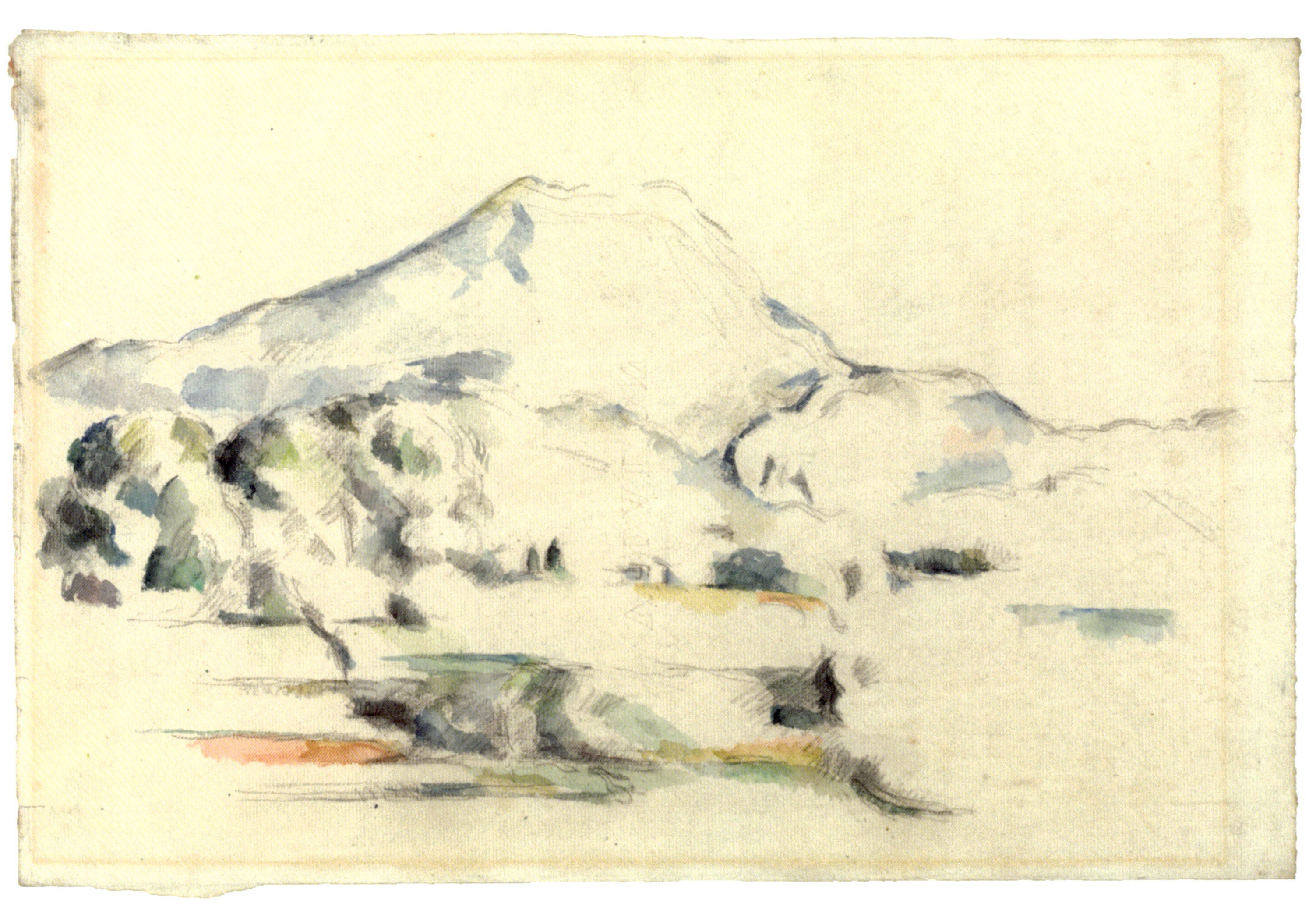

Cat.2
Paul Cezanne (1839–1906)
Paysage provençal (environs de Gardanne?), c.1885
Graphite and watercolour on laid paper, 12⅝ × 19¾ in. (32.1 × 50.3 cm)
Private collection

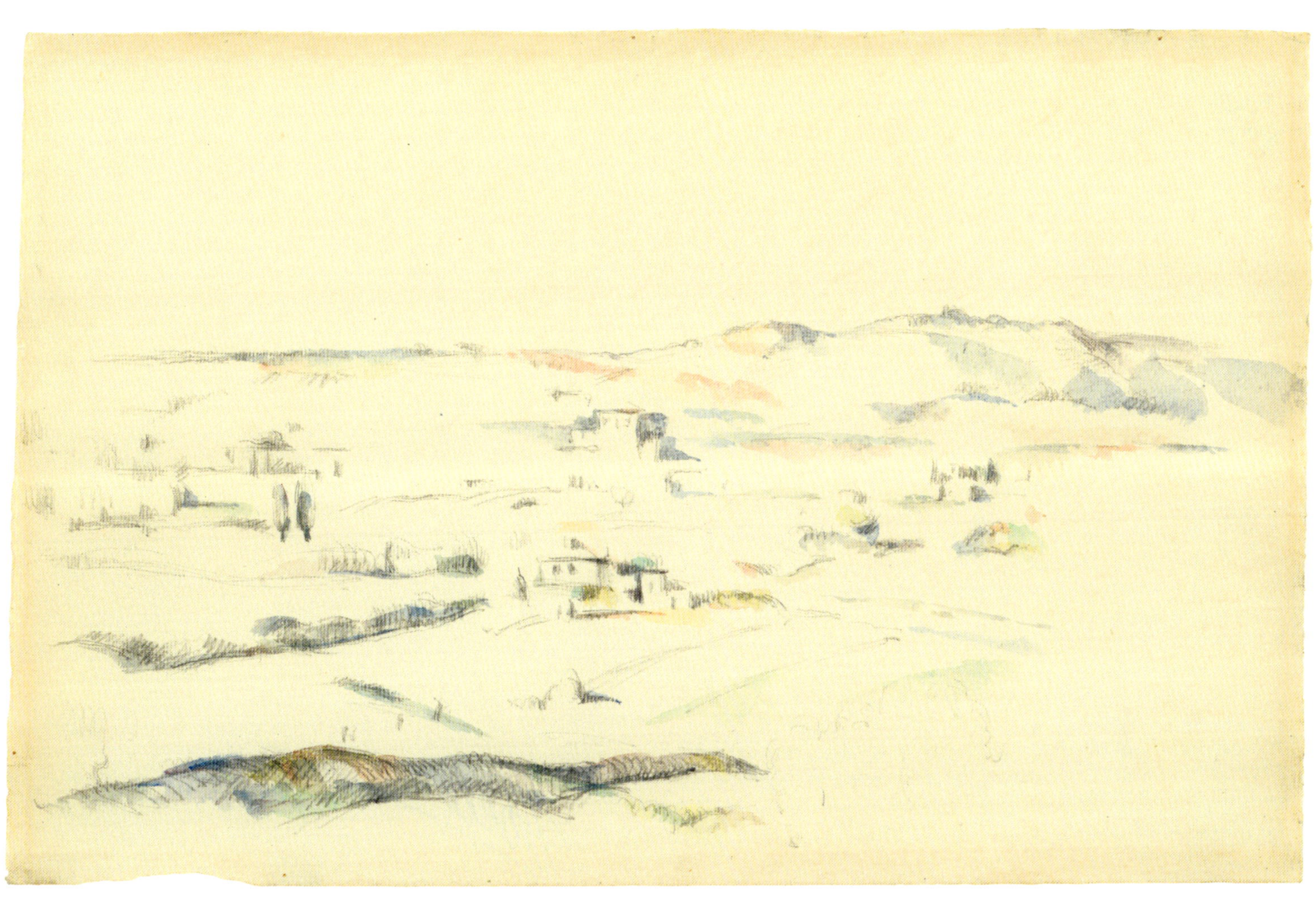

Cat.3
Paul Cezanne (1839–1906)
Rochers près des grottes au-dessus de Château Noir, 1895–1900
Watercolour on laid paper, 19¼ × 11⅜ in. (48.9 × 29 cm)
Private collection

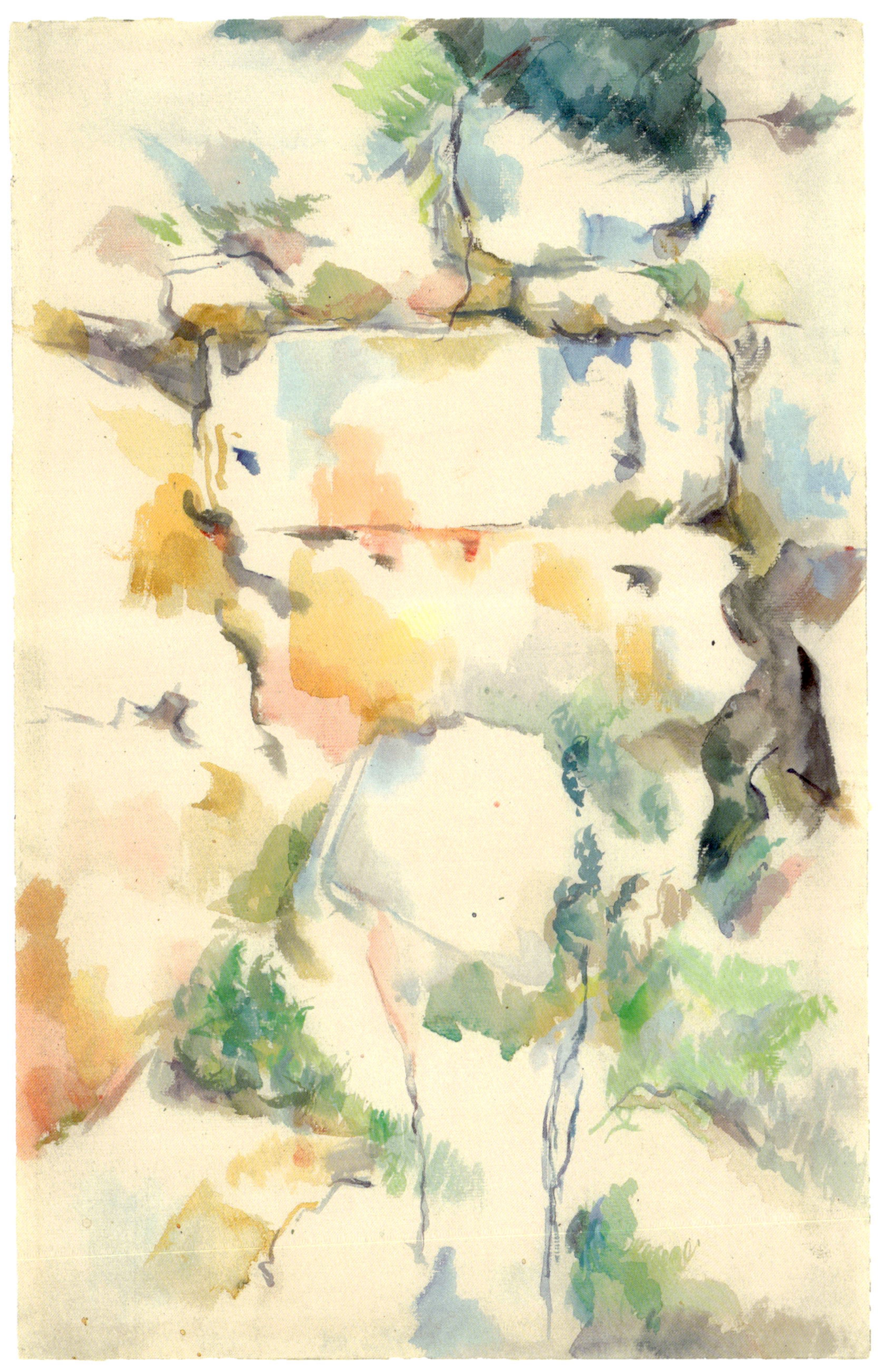

Cat.4
Paul Cezanne (1839–1906)
Rochers et arbres, Bibémus, c.1895
Graphite and watercolour on laid paper, 17⅛ × 14¼ in. (48.8 × 34.4 cm)
Musée Granet, Aix-en-Provence

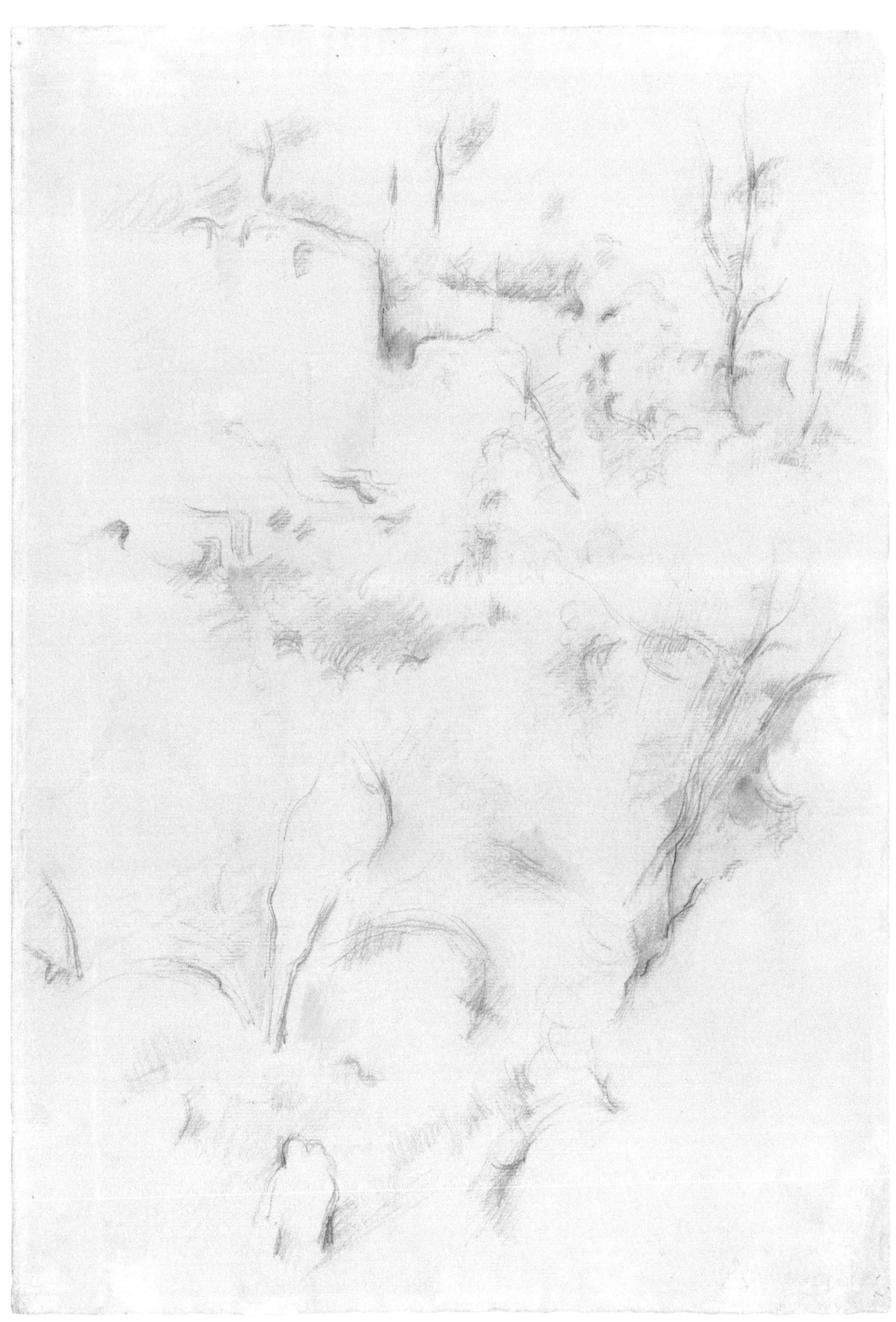

Cats 5a and 5b (verso and recto)
Paul Cezanne (1839–1906)
Verso: *Le Jardin des Lauves*, 1902–06
Recto: *Le Jardin des Lauves: vue sur Aix et la Cathédrale de Saint-Sauveur*, 1902–06
Graphite and watercolour on wove paper, 15¾ × 22 in. (40 × 54 cm)
Private collection

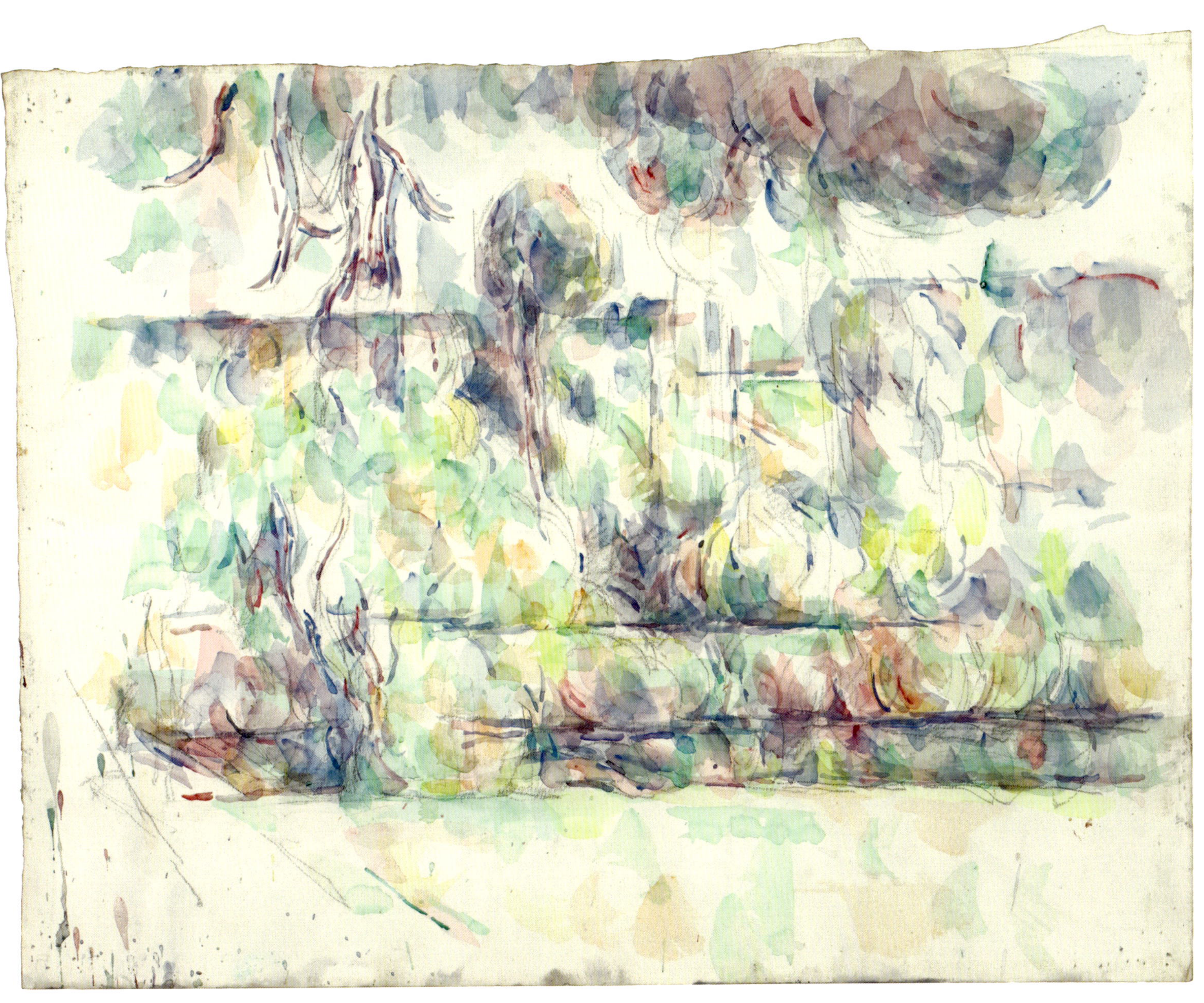

Cat.6
Paul Cezanne (1839–1906)
Route avec arbres sur une pente, c.1904
Watercolour on wove paper, 18⅜ × 13 in. (47.8 × 31.3 cm)
Fondation Beyeler, Riehen/Basel

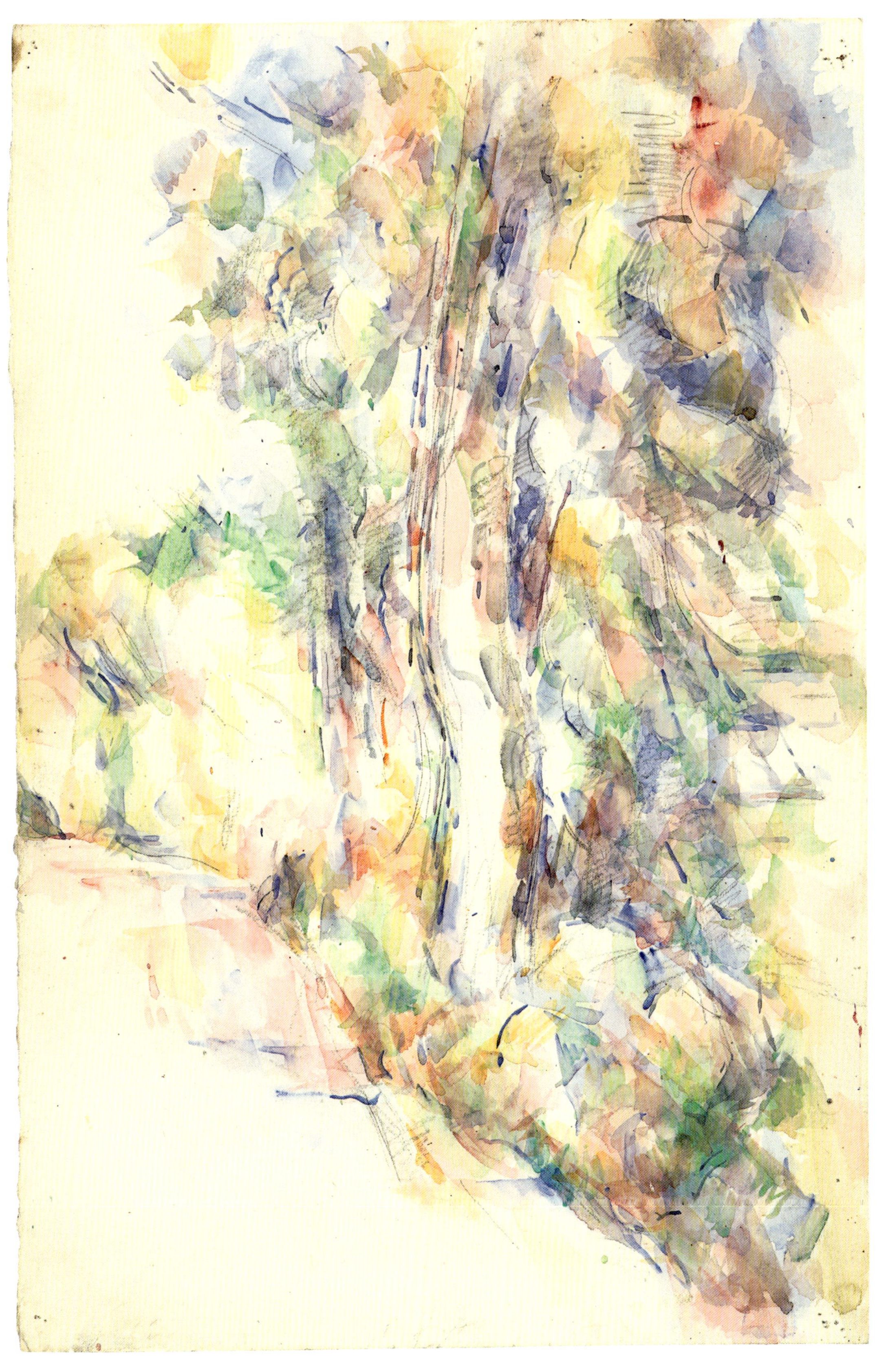

Cat.7
Paul Cezanne (1839–1906)
Paysage provençal, 1885–90
Graphite and watercolour on yellowish laid paper, 12⅝ × 19 in. (32 × 48.3 cm)
Ashmolean Museum, Oxford (Bequest of F. Hindley Smith)

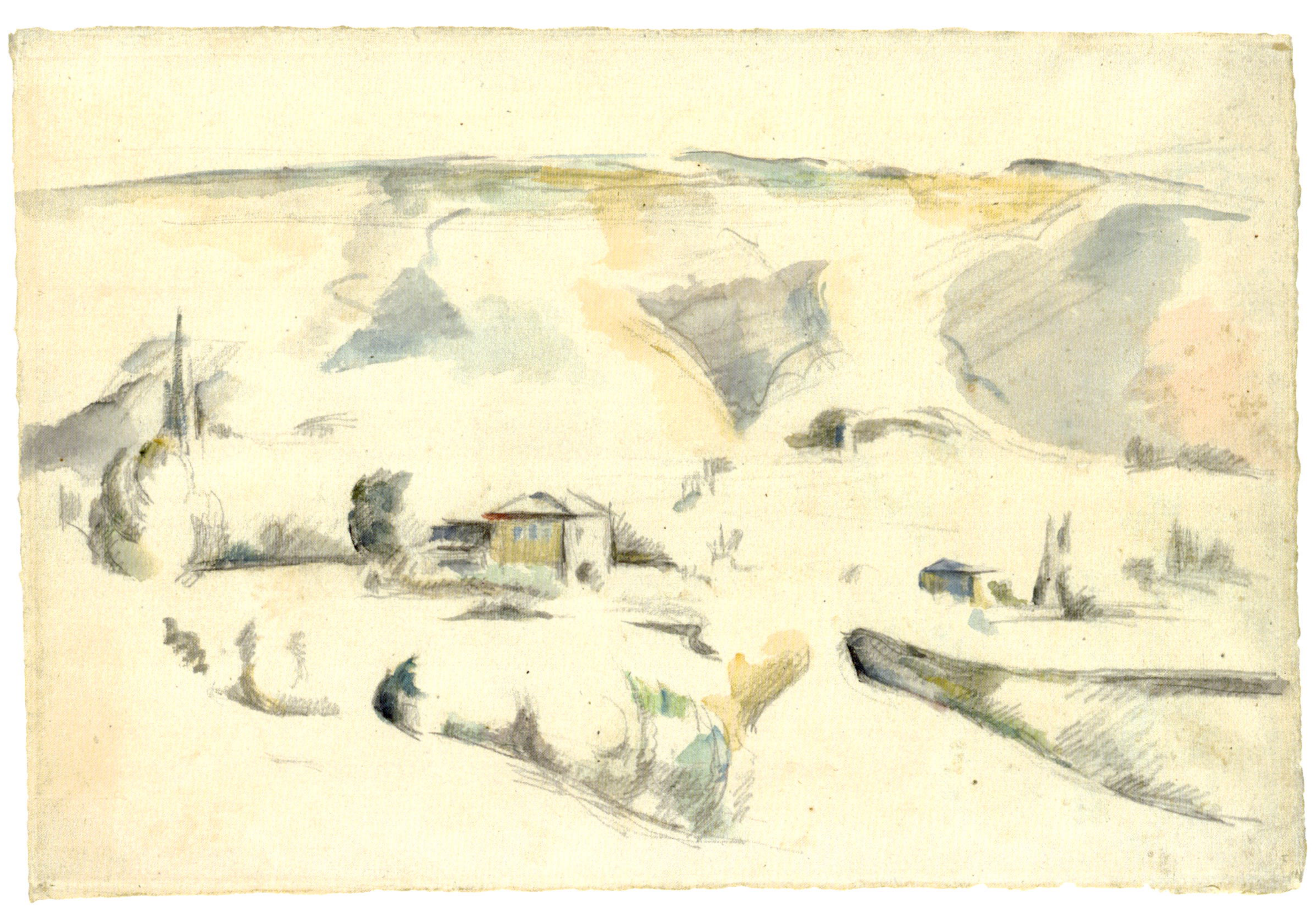

Cat. 8
Paul Cezanne (1839–1906)
Environs de la Sainte-Baume, 1883–86
Graphite on laid paper, 11⁷⁄₁₆ × 18½ in. (30.5 × 48.1 cm)
Private collection

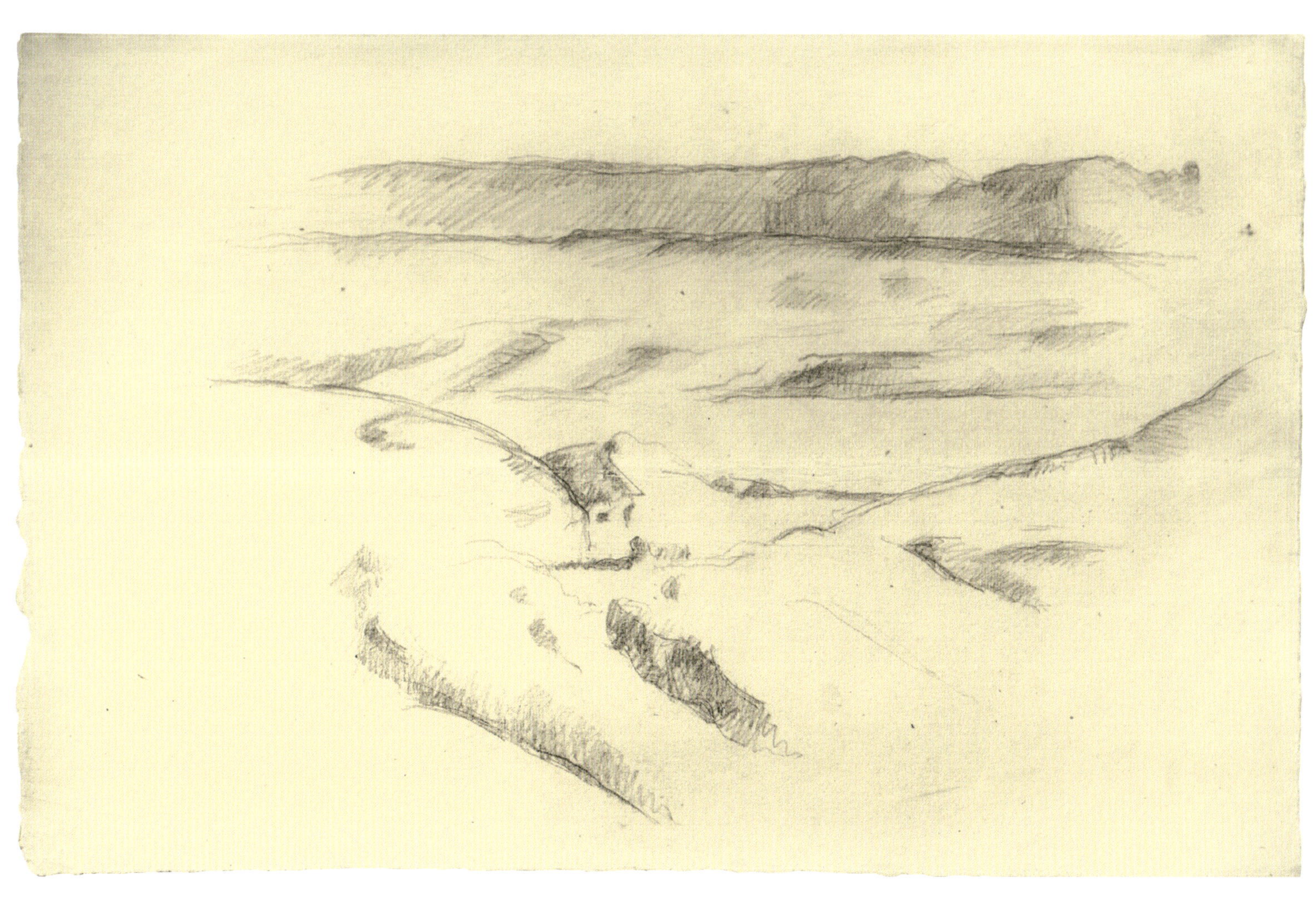

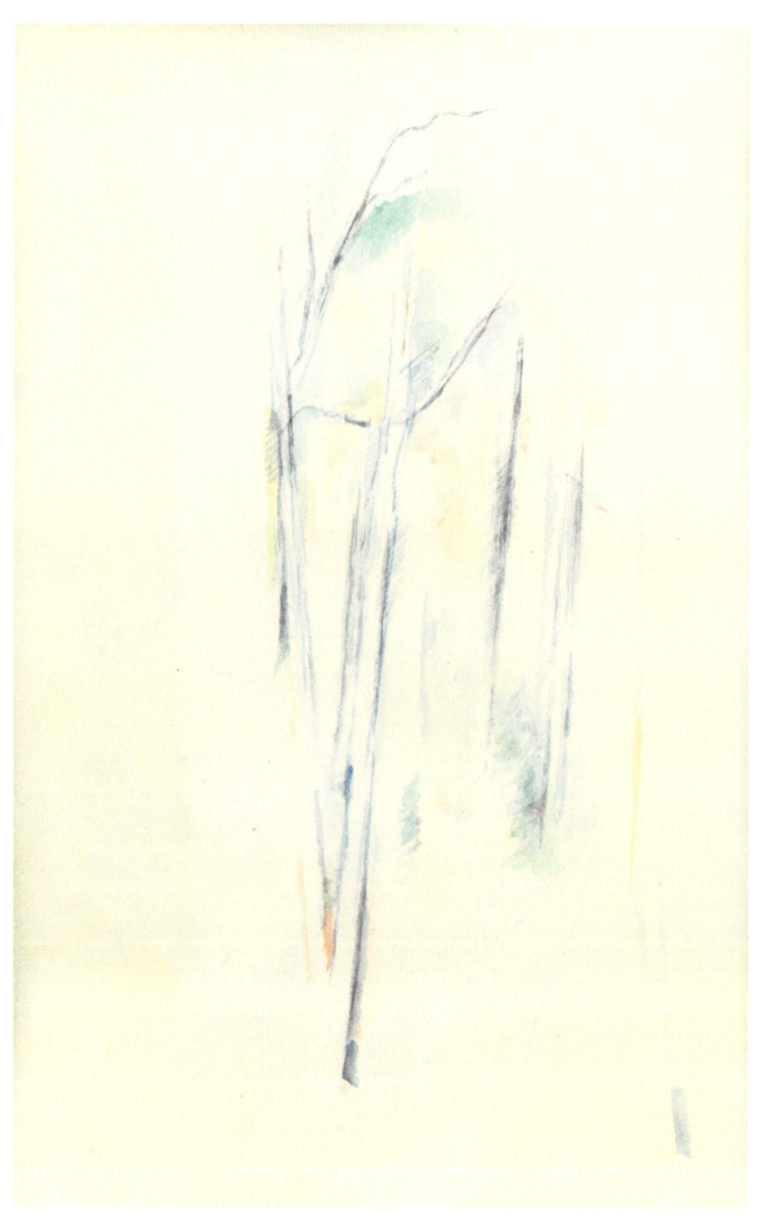

Cats 9a and 9b (verso and recto)
Paul Cezanne (1839–1906)
Verso: *Etude d'arbres*, c.1895–98
Recto: *Dans la forêt, II*, c.1895–98
Graphite and watercolour on wove paper, 17⅝ × 11⅞ in. (44.8 × 30.1 cm)
Private collection

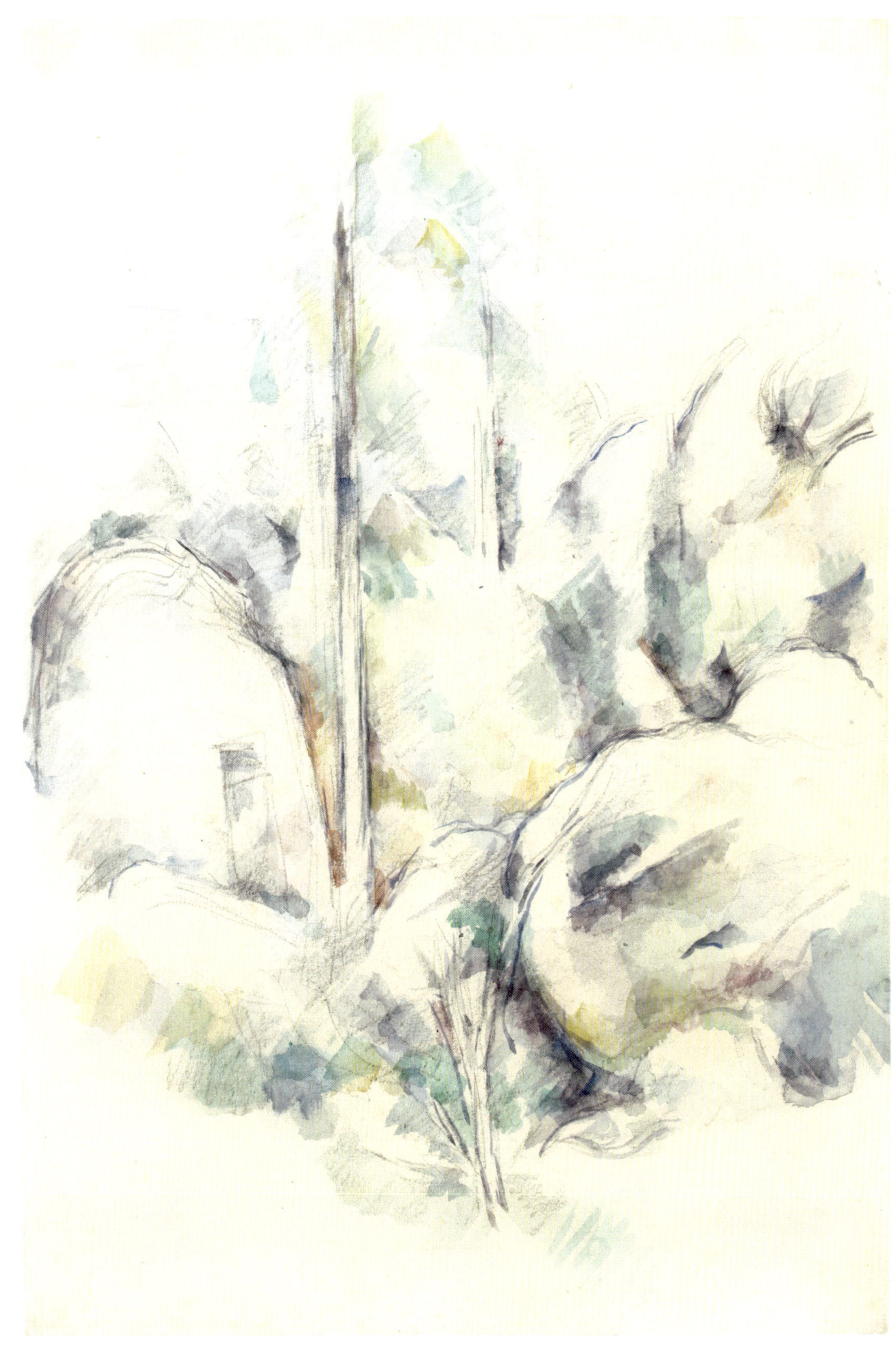

Cat.10
Paul Cezanne (1839–1906)
Sentier en forêt, 1882–84
Graphite and watercolour on laid paper, 18½ × 12¼ in. (47.9 × 31 cm)
Private collection

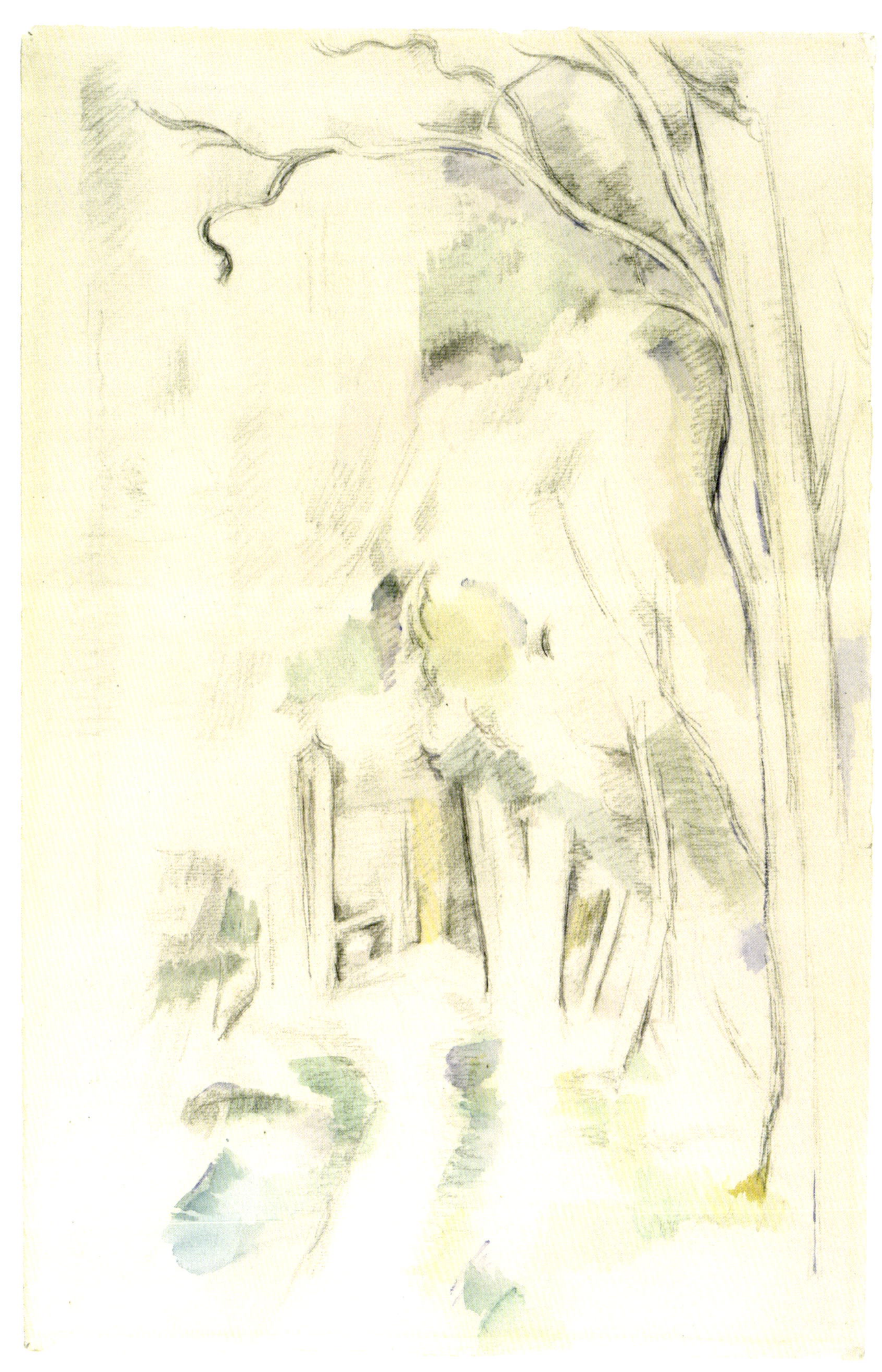

Cat.11
Paul Cezanne (1839–1906)
Arbres et clôture, 1885–88
Graphite on wove paper, 17 × 12⅗ in. (43.5 × 32 cm)
Private collection

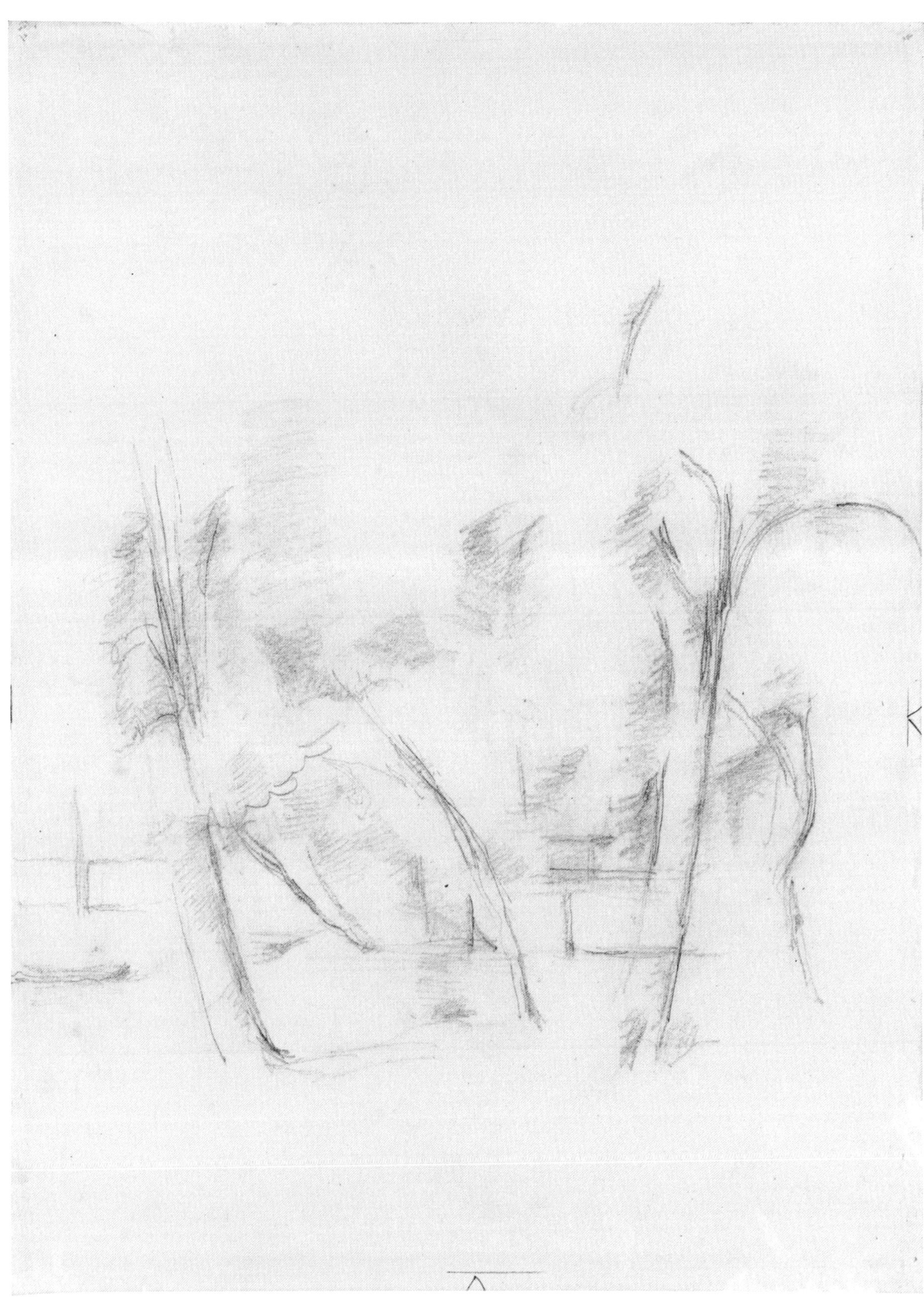

BIBLIOGRAPHY

ANDERSEN 1962
Andersen, Wayne V., 'Cézanne's Sketchbook in the Art Institute of Chicago', *The Burlington Magazine*, vol.104, no.710, May 1962, pp.196–201

ANDERSEN 1965
Andersen, Wayne V., 'Cézanne's Carnet Violet-Moiré', *The Burlington Magazine*, vol.107, no.747, June 1965, pp.312–18

ANDRÉ 1996
André, Louis, *Machines à papier. Innovation et transformations de l'industrie papetière en France 1798–1860*, École des Hautes Études en Sciences Sociales, Paris, 1996

ANDRÉ 2011
André, Louis, 'Les Papiers à dessin, XIXe–XXe siècles', in Natalie Coural, *Le Papier à l'œuvre*, exh. cat., Musée du Louvre, Paris, pp.83–97

ARMSTRONG 2004
Armstrong, Carol, *Cézanne in the Studio: Still Life in Watercolors*, exh. cat., J. Paul Getty Museum, Los Angeles, 2004

ASH AND ZIESKE 2003
Ash, Nancy, and Faith Zieske, 'Looking Closely at Drawing Materials', www.philamuseum.org/booklets/11_67_148_1.html, accessed 25 August 2019

ASH, HOMOLKA AND LUSSIER 2014
Ash, Nancy, Scott Homolka and Stephane Lussier, with Rebecca Pollak and Eliza Spaulding, 'Descriptive Terminology for Works of Art on Paper: Guidelines for the Accurate and Consistent Description of the Materials and Techniques of Drawings, Prints, and Collages', Philadelphia Museum of Art, Philadelphia, www.philamuseum.org/doc_downloads/conservation/DescriptiveTerminologyforArtonPaper.pdf, 2014

BAKER 2010
Baker, Cathleen A., *From the Hand to the Machine – Nineteenth-Century American Paper and Mediums: Technologies, Materials, and Conservation*, Legacy Press, Ann Arbor, MI, 2010

BERTHOLD 1958
Berthold, Gertrude, *Cézanne und die alten Meister. Die Bedeutung der Zeichnungen nach Werken anderer Künstler*, W. Kohlhammer, Stuttgart, 1958

BOWER 1990
Bower, Peter, *Turner's Papers: A Study of the Manufacture, Selection and Use of his Drawing Papers, 1787–1820*, exh. cat., Tate Gallery, London, 1990

BOWER 1999
Bower, Peter, *Turner's Later Papers: A Study of the Manufacture, Selection and Use of his Drawing Papers, 1820–1851*, exh. cat., Tate Gallery, London, 1999

BRIQUET 1907
Briquet, Charles Moïse, *Les Filigranes. Dictionnaire historique des marques du papier dès leur apparition vers 1282 jusqu'en 1600*, 4 vols, A. Jullien, Geneva, 1907

BUCHBERG 2007
Buchberg, Karl, 'Seurat: Materials and Techniques', in Jodi Hauptman (ed), *Georges Seurat: The Drawings*, exh. cat., Museum of Modern Art, New York, 2007, pp.31–4

BUCK, HOUSE, VEGELIN VAN CLAERBERGEN AND WRIGHT 2008
Buck, Stephanie, John House, Ernst Vegelin van Claerbergen and Barnaby Wright (eds), *The Courtauld Cézannes*, exh. cat., Courtauld Gallery, London, 2008

BURNSTOCK, HALE, CAMPBELL AND MACARO 2010
Burnstock, Aviva, Charlotte Hale, Caroline Campbell and Gabriella Macaro, 'Cézanne's Development of the Card Players', in Ireson and Wright 2010, pp.35–53

BUTLER 1984
Marigene H. Butler, *An Investigation of the Materials and Technique Used by Paul Cézanne*, Amercian Institute of Conservation of Historic and Artistic Works, Preprints of Papers Presented at the Twelfth Annual Meeting, Los Angeles, 15–20 May 1984, pp.20–33

CHAPPUIS 1966
Chappuis, Adrien, *Album de Paul Cézanne*,
preface by Roseline Bacou, 2 vols,
Berggruen, Paris, 1966

CHAPPUIS 1973
Chappuis, Adrien, *The Drawings of Paul
Cézanne: A Catalogue Raisonné*, 2 vols, New
York Graphic Society, Greenwich, CT, 1973

DORAN 1978
Doran, Michael (ed), *Conversations avec
Cézanne*, Éditions Macula, Paris, 1978

EILING 2017
Eiling, Alexander (ed), *Cézanne:
Metamorphoses*, exh. cat., Kunsthalle
Karlsruhe, Karlsruhe, 2017

ELDERFIELD 2017
Elderfield, John, with Mary Morton and
Xavier Rey, *Paul Cézanne: The Portraits*,
exh. cat., Musée d'Orsay, Paris, National
Portrait Gallery, London, and National
Gallery of Art, Washington DC, 2017

FEILCHENFELDT 1996
Feilchenfeldt, Walter, 'On Sizes and
Subjects', in Rewald 1996, pp.16–17

FEILCHENFELDT, WARMAN
AND NASH 2014
Feilchenfeldt, Walter, Jayne Warman
and David Nash, *The Paintings of Paul
Cézanne: An Online Catalogue Raisonné*,
www.cezannecatalogue.com/catalogue/
index.php

GASKELL 1972
Gaskell, Philip, *A New Introduction to
Bibliography*, Clarendon Press, Oxford, 1972

GAUDRIAULT 1995
Gaudriault, Raymond, with Thérèse
Gaudriault, *Filigranes et autres
caractéristiques des papiers fabriqués en France
aux XVIIe et XVIIIe siècles*, CNRS Éditions,
Paris, 1995

HALDEMANN 2017
Haldemann, Anita (ed), *The Hidden
Cézanne: From Sketchbook to Canvas*, exh. cat.,
Kunstmuseum Basel, Basel, 2017

HALE 2014
Hale, Charlotte, 'A Template for
Experimentation: Cézanne's Process and
the Paintings of Hortense Fiquet', in Dita
Amory (ed.), *Madame Cézanne*, exh. cat.,
Metropolitan Museum of Art, New York,
2014, pp.45–71

HUNTER 1957
Hunter, Dard, *Papermaking: The History and
Technique of an Ancient Craft*, The Cresset
Press, London, 1957

IRESON AND WRIGHT 2010
Ireson, Nancy, and Barnaby Wright (eds),
Cézanne's Card Players, exh. cat., Courtauld
Gallery, London, and Metropolitan
Museum of Art, New York, 2010

KEMP 1974
Kemp, Wolfgang, 'Disegno. Beiträge
zur Geschichte des Begriffs zwischen
1547 und 1607', *Marburger Jahrbuch für
Kunstwissenschaft*, vol. 19, 1974, pp.219–40

LOEBER 1982
Loeber, E. G., *Paper Mould and Mouldmaker*,
Paper Publications Society, Amsterdam,
1982

MEEDENDORP 2007
Meedendorp, Teio, *Drawings and Prints
by Vincent van Gogh in the Collection of
the Kröller-Müller Museum*, Thieme Art,
Deventer, 2007

MONNIER 1977
Monnier, Geneviève, 'The Late
Watercolors', in William Rubin (ed),
Cézanne: The Late Work, exh. cat., Museum
of Modern Art, New York, 1977, pp.113–18

MOTZ 2019
Wach, Alexandra, Anna Motz, 'Schmaler
Grat zwischen Spur und Schaden.
Gespräch mit Städel-Restauratorin Anna
Motz über den einmaligen Bestand an
Skizzenbüchern', *Restauro. Zeitschrift für
Konservierung und Restaurierung*, vol.125,
no.4, June 2019, pp.56–61

PAPER SAMPLE COLLECTION
Paper Sample Collection, Paper
Conservation, National Gallery of Art,
Washington DC
www.nga.gov/conservation/paper-sample.
html, accessed 15 March 2017

RATCLIFFE 1960
Ratcliffe, Robert W., 'Cézanne's
Working Methods and their Theoretical
Background', PhD thesis, Courtauld
Institute of Art, University of London,
1960

REFF AND SHOEMAKER 1989
Reff, Theodore, and Innis Howe
Shoemaker, *Paul Cézanne: Two Sketchbooks –
The Gift of Mr. and Mrs. Walter H. Annenberg
to the Philadelphia Museum of Art*, exh.
cat., Philadelphia Museum of Art,
Philadelphia, 1989

REFF 1958
Reff, Theodore, 'Studies in the Drawings
of Cézanne', PhD thesis, Harvard
University, Cambridge, MA, 1958

REFF 1960
Reff, Theodore, 'Review: *Gertrude Berthold.
Cézanne und die Alten Meister*', *The Art
Bulletin*, vol.42, no.2, June 1960, pp.145–49

REISSNER 2008A
Reissner, Elisabeth, 'Ways of Making:
Practice and Innovation in Cézanne's
Paintings in the National Gallery', *National
Gallery Technical Bulletin*, vol.29, 2008,
pp.4–30

REISSNER 2008B
Reissner, Elisabeth, 'Transparency
of Means: "Drawing" and Colour in
Cézanne's Watercolours and Oil Paintings
in The Courtauld Gallery', in Buck, House,
Vegelin van Claerbergen and Wright 2008,
pp.48–71

REWALD 1937
Rewald, John, *Paul Cézanne: Correspondance*,
Grasset, Paris, 1937

REWALD 1951
Rewald, John, *Paul Cézanne: Carnets de
dessins*, 2 vols, Paris, 1951

REWALD 1982
Rewald, John, *Paul Cézanne: Sketchbook,
1875–1885*, trans. Olivier Bernier, 2 vols,
New York, 1982

REWALD 1983
Rewald, John, *Paul Cézanne: The Watercolours, a Catalogue Raisonné*, Thames & Hudson, London, 1983

REWALD 1984
Rewald, John (ed), *Paul Cézanne: Letters*, trans. Seymour Hacker, revd edn, Hacker Art Books, New York, 1984

REWALD 1996
Rewald, John, with Walter Feilchenfeldt and Jayne Warman, *The Paintings of Paul Cézanne: A Catalogue Raisonné*, 2 vols, Abrams, New York, 1996

REWALD AND MARSCHUTZ 1935
Rewald, John, and Léo Marschutz, 'Plastique et réalité. Cézanne au Château Noir', *L'Amour de l'art*, vol.16, 1935, pp.15–21

REYNAUD 1989
Reynaud, Marie-Hélène, *Une histoire de papier. Les papeteries Canson et Montgolfier* Canson, Annonay, 1989

RUPPEN 2017A
Ruppen, Fabienne, 'Reassembling Cézanne: Material Evidence for a New Sketchbook', *Master Drawings*, vol.55, no.2, Summer 2017, pp.211–24

RUPPEN 2017B
Ruppen, Fabienne, 'Paul Cézanne's Loose Sheets in the Kupferstichkabinett of the Kunstmuseums Basel', in Haldemann 2017, pp.220–31

RUPPEN 2017C
Ruppen, Fabienne, 'On Margins and Versos: The Hidden Interrelationships among Cézanne's Works on Paper', in Eiling 2017, pp.84–99

RUPPEN 2018
Ruppen, Fabienne, 'Der fragmentierte Cézanne. Skizzenbücher und lose Blätter', PhD thesis, University of Zurich, 2018

RUPPEN 2019
Ruppen, Fabienne, 'Mapping Cézanne: Drawings and Watercolors on Paper from Emile Desloye', *Actes de journée d'étude: Le filigrane, une marque à explorer*, HiCSA, Paris, 2019 (forthcoming)

SCHENCK 2005
Schenck, Kimberly, 'Crayon, Paper, and Paint: An Examination of Nineteenth-Century Drawing Materials', in Jay McKean Fisher et al., *The Essence of Line: French Drawings from Ingres to Degas*, Pennsylvania State University Press, University Park, PA, 2005, pp.57–79

SCHNIEWIND 1951
Schniewind, Carl O., *Paul Cézanne: Sketch Book Owned by the Art Institute of Chicago*, 2 vols, Curt Valentin, New York, 1951

SCHUBERT 2006
Schubert, Karsten, 'Cézanne, Chappuis and the Limits of Connoisseurship', *The Burlington Magazine*, vol.148, no.1242, September 2006, pp.612–20

SEGER 2017
Seger, Annegret, 'The Reconstruction of the Basel Sketchbooks of Paul Cézanne', in Haldemann 2017, pp.232–39

SENNELIER 1904
Sennelier, G., *Catalogue général illustré de G. Sennelier, fabricant de couleurs fines, matériel d'artistes*, no.26, 1904

SHELLEY 2014
Shelley, Marjorie, 'Cézanne as Draftsman: Sketchbooks and Graphite Drawings', in Dita Amory, *Madame Cézanne*, exh. cat., Metropolitan Museum of Art, New York, 2014, pp.107–27

SHOEMAKER 1989
Shoemaker, Innis Howe, 'The Philadelphia Sketchbooks, Past and Present', in Reff and Shoemaker 1989, pp.15–26

SIMMS 2008
Simms, Matthew, *Cézanne's Watercolors: Between Drawing and Painting*, Yale University Press, New Haven, CT, and London, 2008

STEVENSON 1961
Stevenson, Allan, *Observations on Paper as Evidence*, University of Kansas Publications, Lawrence, KS, 1961

STEWART 2014
Stewart, Miriam, 'Curating Sketchbooks: Interpretation, Preservation, Display', in Angela Bartram, Nader El-Bizri and Douglas Gittens (eds), *Recto Verso: Redefining the Sketchbook*, Ashgate, Farnham, 2014, pp.163–75

TSCHUDIN 2007
Tschudin, Peter F., *Grundzüge der Papiergeschichte*, Anton Hiersemann, Stuttgart, 2007

VENTURI 1936
Venturi, Lionello, *Cézanne. Son art – son œuvre*, 2 vols, Paul Rosenberg, Paris, 1936

WASSERZEICHEN-INFORMATIONS-SYSTEM (WZIS)
www.wasserzeichen-online.de/wzis/index.php (in German, accessed 27 May 2019)

WHITELEY 2000
Whiteley, Jon, Catalogue of the Collection of Drawings in the Ashmolean Museum, vol.7: *French School*, Oxford University Press, Oxford, 2000

ZENDER 2008
Zender, Joachim Elias, *Lexikon Buch, Druck, Papier*, Haupt, Bern, Stuttgart and Vienna, 2008

ZIESKE 1992
Zieske, Faith, 'The Conservation of Two Sketchbooks by Paul Cézanne', in Sheila Fairbrass (ed), *International Institute of Paper Conservation: Conference Papers, Manchester 1992*, papers presented to the third International Institute of Paper Conservation Conference at the University of Manchester, Institute of Science and Technology, London, 1992, pp.54–60

ZIESKE 2002
Zieske, Faith, 'Paul Cézanne's Watercolors: His Choice of Pigments and Papers', in Harriet K. Stratis and Britt Salvesen, *The Broad Spectrum: Studies in the Materials, Techniques, and Conservation of Color on Paper*, Archetype Publications, London, 2002, pp.89–100

This publication follows the decision of the Société Paul Cezanne
and the campaign of Philippe Paul Cezanne, the great-grandson
of the artist, to spell the artist's name without an acute accent.
This decision has been carried forward in the new online catalogue
raisonné of the artist, under the direction of Walter Feilchenfeldt,
Jayne Warman and David Nash, as well as in other recent
publications such as *Cezanne Jas de Bouffan – Art et histoire* (Fage
Éditions). They argue that Cezanne, when writing letters or signing
pictures, never wrote his name with an accent. In Provençal, the
letter 'e' is pronounced the same way as the e-acute in French. The
accented spelling of Cezanne's name was gradually adopted by his
wife, Hortense Fiquet (but not until the 1890s), and by Paul Cezanne
fils, possibly to make it clear to Parisians and other non-Provençaux
how the name should be pronounced. This will be one of the first
publications to follow the ruling of the Société Paul Cezanne to
drop the accent.

Published in 2019 by
Ridinghouse and
Luxembourg & Dayan, London

on the occasion of the exhibition
*Reconstructing Cezanne: Sequence and Process
in Paul Cezanne's Works on Paper*
at Luxembourg & Dayan
2 October–7 December 2019

Luxembourg & Dayan
2 Savile Row, London W1S 3PA
United Kingdom
luxembourgdayan.com

Ridinghouse
46 Lexington Street
London W1F 0LP
United Kingdom
ridinghouse.co.uk

Distributed in the UK and Europe by
Cornerhouse Publications
c/o Home
2 Tony Wilson Place
Manchester M15 4FN
United Kingdom
cornerhousepublications.org

Distributed in the United States and
    Canada by
ARTBOOK | D.A.P.
75 Broad Street, Suite 630
New York, New York 10004
artbook.com

Texts © Yuval Etgar, Walter Feilchenfeldt
    and Fabienne Ruppen
For the book in this form © Ridinghouse
    and Luxembourg & Dayan

British Library Cataloguing-in-
    Publication Data
A full catalogue record of this book is
    available from the British Library.

ISBN 978 1 909932 55 5

Ridinghouse Publisher: Sophie Kullmann
Edited by Sophie Kullmann
Exhibition coordination: Inès Leynaud
Translation: Martina Dervis

Designed by Mark Thomson
Set in Lexicon (Bram de Does)

Printed in Belgium by die Keure

LUXEMBOURG & DAYAN

Ridinghouse